A SHORT H

A Short History of Japan

Ernest Wilson Clement

AERANOVA

CONTENTS

PREFACE

The object of this book is to give a bird's-eye view of the history of Japan,[1] and to indicate in outline how both Old Japan and New Japan were constructed and evolved. It is believed that many persons who would not care to go into the details of Japanese history would like to get an epitome, a general idea, of what has happened during the long course of the history of Japan, Old and New. This book may, therefore, be sufficient for the purposes of that individual known as the "average reader." And, as frequent references are made to fuller accounts, it may also be an introduction to Japanese history for those who desire to pursue the study farther. It should, perhaps, be added that the history of Japan is both interesting and instructive: it is full of the most romantic and exciting incidents and episodes, and it is a study in the evolution of a wonderful people who have astonished the world.

The author does not lay claim to originality; he has made use of all materials at hand and has given credit where credit is due. He has, however, applied his own interpretations to the historical and other events recorded and has tried to portray their meaning and their bearing, especially upon the evolution of Japan.

There is no attempt at absolute uniformity in the transliteration of Japanese words, nor is there so much variety as to confuse. There is not much practical difference between Tōkiō and Tōkyō; Ieyasu and Iyeyasu; Kiū-shiu, Kyū-shiu, Kiū-shū, Kyū-shū; though there is more divergence between Riūkiū, Liūkiū, Luchu, Loo Choo, Lew Chew. But the distinction between the long and the short vowels (o and ō, u and ū) is very

---

[1] Up to the end of the Meiji Era in 1912.

important.

For permission to use material contained in his own *Handbook of Modern Japan* (A. C. McClurg & Co., Chicago) and *Christianity in Modern Japan* (American Baptist Publication Society, Philadelphia) the author wishes here to express his thanks to the publishers.

The author has tried to be accurate but may have made mistakes, for the correction of which he will be thankful. He will be quite satisfied if this little book becomes a guide in the study of the history of Japan.

ERNEST WILSON CLEMENT

July 1, 1915

JAPANESE PRONUNCIATION

a – a *in father*	i – *i in pin*	*u* – oo *in book*
ai *as in aisle*	au – o *in bone*	ū – oo *in moon*
e – e *in men*	*o* – o *in pony*	
ei *as in weigh*	ō – oo *in moon*	

i in the middle of a word and *u* in the middle or at the end of a word are sometimes almost inaudible.

The consonants are all sounded, as in English: *g,* however, has only the hard sound, as in *give,* although the nasal *ng* is often heard; *ch* and *s* are always soft, as in *check* and *sin;* and *z* before *u* has the sound of *dz.* In the case of double consonants, each one must be given its full sound.

There are as many syllables as vowels. There is practically no accent; but care must be taken to distinguish between *o* and ō, *u* and ū, of which the second is more prolonged than the first.

Be sure to avoid the flat sound of *a;* it is always pronounced *ah.*

Japanese words, especially names, should almost always be divided into syllables with a vowel at the end of each syllable. The principal exception is in the case of double consonants; then the syllabic division is made between the two consonants: *n* may also close a syllable.

CHAPTER I. INTRODUCTION: THE DIVINE AGES

The student of Japanese history is confronted at the outset with a serious difficulty. In ancient times the Japanese had no literary script, so that all events had to be handed down from generation to generation by oral tradition. Moreover, the early records made after the introduction of the art of writing were destroyed by fire, so that the only "reliance or information about... antiquity" has to be placed in the *Kojiki* ("Records of Ancient Matters")[1] and in the *Nihongi* ("Chronicles of Japan")[2]. The former, completed in 712 A.D., is written in a purer Japanese style; while the latter, finished in 720 A.D., is "much more tinctured with Chinese philosophy": though differing in some details, they are practically concordant and supply the data upon which Japanese "history" has been constructed.

In accordance with our present purpose, it seems best, following the illustrious example of Arnold in Roman history, to treat the more or less mythological periods in the form in which they have been handed down in tradition, and thus preserve "the spirit of the people," as reflected in the legends. As Dr. Murray puts it, "Yet the events of the earlier period which have been preserved for us by oral tradition are capable, with due care and inspection, of furnishing important lessons and disclosing many facts in regard to the lives and characteristics of the primitive Japanese."[3] Therefore, without attempting to indulge specially in "higher criticism," which has not yet accomplished its much-needed work in the field of Japanese history, we shall rather endeavor to present that history, so far as possible, in Japanese dress and from the Japanese point of view. And we must surely

---

[1] See *Transactions of the Asiatic Society of Japan*, Vol. X, Supplement.

[2] See Supplement, *Proceedings of the Japan Society*, London.

[3] Japan, in "The Story of the Nations" series.

admit the continuity of Japanese history as illustrated in the "unbroken line of illustrious sovereigns," who, for at least eighteen or twenty centuries, have formed the oldest continuous dynasty in the world. Another point of extraordinary importance is that, in all the history of Japan since the beginning, the country "has never once felt the shame of foreign conquest." And this unusual fact is regarded by many as an indubitable proof, not merely of the "divine right," but also of the "divine descent," of the Japanese emperors. "To the end of time each Mikado is the son of the [sun-] goddess." The spirit of the divine ancestors still holds sway. Although Charles I of England paid with his life the penalty of insisting too vigorously and too practically upon the exemplification of the theory of "the divine right of the king," no Stuart ever even dreamed of the applications to which it could be put in Japan. And the theory of divinity extended also to the land itself; for a Japanese poet (Hitomaro) once wrote the following lines:

Japan is not a land where men need pray,
For it's itself divine.

There are various plans by which we may portion off Japanese history. In a very general way, we may make the following three divisions:

Ancient: Imperialism (patriarchal).
Mediaeval: Feudalism (military).
Modern: Imperialism (constitutional).

Brinkley, in his encyclopedic work,[1] writes as follows:

There are, in fact, six great divisions of Japanese
history: first, the patriarchal age, when the sovereign
was only the head of a group of tribal chiefs, each

---

[1] *Japan: Its History, Arts and Literature*, I, 173.

> possessing a hereditary share of the governing power;
> secondly, a brief period, from the middle of the
> seventh to the early part of the eighth century, when
> the tribal chiefs had disappeared and the Throne was
> approximately autocratic; thirdly, an interval of
> some eighty years, called the Nara Epoch, during
> which the propagandism of Buddhism and the
> development of the material and artistic civilization
> that came in that religious train engrossed the
> attention of the nation; fourthly, the Heian Epoch, a
> period of three centuries, when the Court in Kyōto
> ruled vicariously through the Fujiwara family; fifthly,
> the age of military feudalism, from the beginning of
> the twelfth to the middle of the nineteenth century,
> when the administrative power was grasped by
> soldier nobles; and sixthly, the present, or Meiji
> Epoch, of constitutional monarchy.

Another plan, however, which is more particular and definite, suits our purpose better; but its delimitations must not be taken too literally or its chronology too precisely. Dates will be added, not alone for accuracy, but sometimes merely for convenience. The following is the plan:

OLD JAPAN
The Divine Ages
The Prehistoric Period
The Imperialistic Period
The Heian Epoch (Fujiwara Bureaucracy)
The Gempei Era
Hōjō Tyranny
Ashikaga Anarchy
Civil Strife
Tokugawa Feudalism

In the case of New Japan, it is possible, in the very names of the periods, to trace the progress of the last sixty years (1853-1913).

THE "DIVINE AGES" (BEFORE 660 [?] B.C.)

From the point of view of the historical critic there is no break between this period and the next, so that the two might fairly be combined under the title "*Prehistoric*." But this first period is quite distinct in the minds of Japanese and is called in their histories *Jindai*, which means "*Divine Ages*." It is acknowledged, in the official *History of the Empire of Japan*, that "strange and incredible legends have been transmitted from that era"; but it is added that, "in order to understand the history of the Empire's beginnings, the traditional incidents of the age, however singular, must be studied." There is also another reason why some attention should be given to the myths and legends of this unhistorical period. The incidents and the names of the actors are so inextricably interwoven into the fabric of Japanese art, religion, and literature, and are so influential yet among the common people and even in politics, that one cannot afford to ignore this period. Indeed, "the age of the gods and the present [modern] age are not two ages but one"; for all, rulers and ruled,

13

"act upon the traditions of the divine age."[1] It is to be regretted that the legendary nature of this period prevents giving definite dates; for on this point not one of the eight hundred myriads of deities (*yaoyorozu no kami*) has vouchsafed a revelation. The story of the creation of the world bears striking resemblance to that related in Ovid *Metamorphoses*, and has points in common with the story in Genesis. We quote the opening lines of the *Nihongi*, as follows:

> *Of old, Heaven and Earth were not yet separated,*
> *and the male and female principles not yet divided.*
> *They formed a chaotic mass, like an egg, which was*
> *of obscurely defined limits and contained germs. The*
> *purer and clearer part was thinly drawn out and*
> *formed Heaven, while the heavier and grosser*
> *element settled down and became Earth. The finer*
> *element easily became a united body, but the*
> *consolidation of the heavy and gross element was*
> *accomplished with difficulty. Heaven was therefore*
> *formed first and Earth was established subsequently.*
> *Thereafter Divine Beings were produced between*
> *them... At this time a certain thing was produced*
> *between Heaven and Earth. It was in form like a*
> *reed-shoot. Now this became transformed into a God.*

Then various other gods were spontaneously created, at first "solitary males"; but finally five pairs of brothers and sisters were created. The last pair were instructed by the other gods to "make, consolidate, and give birth to the floating land." The dual progenitors, Izanagi and Izanami, in their various activities remind one of Saturn and Rhea, or Jupiter and Juno, or Adam and Eve. The story of Amaterasu, the sun-goddess, provoked by

---

[1] Reed, *Japan*, I, 36.

her boisterous brother, Susano-ō, retiring to a cavern, thus leaving the world in darkness, and finally being enticed out again by a shrewd appeal to curiosity and jealousy, is apparently a myth of a solar eclipse. And one Japanese writer (Kawakami) thinks it "not improbable that the prehistoric tribes of Japan worshipped the sun as the highest deity."

The aforementioned Susano-ō, having finally been expelled from heaven on account of his violent performances, came to Izumo. Here, just as Hercules killed the hydra, Susano-ō kills an eight-forked serpent, from whom he rescues a maiden and takes her as his wife. The cycle of myths clustering about Izumo evidently describe an emigration from Korea into Japan. Still another cycle of myths concerning Ninigi, grandson of the sun goddess, cluster around Tsukushi in Kiūshiu and probably describe a Malay emigration from the south. It was to Ninigi that the heavenly deities entrusted the rosary of jewels (one red, one white, and one blue), the mirror with which the sun-goddess had been enticed from her retirement, and the double-edged sword which Susano-ō had found in the tail of the serpent. These have since been known as the "Three Imperial Insignia." And "they symbolize courage, knowledge, and mercy, the necessary attributes of a great sovereign, of whose divine rights the Regalia are the outward manifestation."[1] The jealousy and quarreling between Ninigi's sons, Prince Fire-Shine and Prince Fire-Fade, are, of course, reminders of Romulus and Remus and of Cain and Abel.

The grandson of Prince Fire-Fade led an emigration, by gradual steps, from Kiūshiu up the main island, until they finally reached a spot, apparently near Ōsaka, then known as Naniwa. In this central section of Japan, the immigrants, or invaders, met opposition from natives; and concerning these events there is a

---

[1] Longford, *Story of Old Japan*.

Yamato cycle of legends.

Finally, when the leader of this expedition had subdued his enemies, he set up his palace at Kashiwabara in the province of Yamato. This event is taken as the beginning of Japanese "history," and has been assigned chronologically to 660 B.C. The aforementioned prince is now known as the Emperor Jimmu, the founder of the Empire of Japan. If he is a truly historical personage, his ascension to the throne can scarcely have been at so early a date as is claimed: but at any rate he is an important "character" and cannot be entirely ignored.

The myths and legends of the "Divine Ages" and the following period have more or less pedagogical value and teach considerable about the native or primitive civilization of the Japanese. Their food, clothing, huts, arms, and implements are all described. They had knowledge of some plants and of some wild and domestic animals. They "had a rude system of agriculture and knew the art of fashioning iron." The family was "in its most rudimentary stage." The people "were able to count only to ten," and were "without writing or commerce" or art. Their mode of government seems to have been a kind of patriarchal feudalistic imperialism. They loved nature, and were full of superstition; they had "childlike religious ideas," with reverential worship, sacrifices, and festivals. Their gods were "only men of prowess or renown."

We ought at least to treat a little, but not minutely, the topics of the Stone Age, the Bronze Age, and the Iron Age in Japan. These eras fall chiefly in the "Divine Ages," but may lap over somewhat into the next period. Various stone implements have been found in different parts of Japan so widely separated as Yezo, the vicinity of Yedo, and Kiūshiu. Milne and Munro[1]

---

[1] See papers in *Transactions of the Asiatic Society of Japan*, Vols. VIII, X, and XXXIV.

assign them to the Ainu, but the best Japanese authorities are inclined to attribute them largely, if not wholly, to a pre-Ainu people known as Koro-pok-guru. This name points out the fact that they lived in pits or caves, and hints that they may possibly be identical with the "earth-spiders" of the *Kojiki*. But one branch of the ancestors of the Japanese proper buried their dead in barrows, in which "are found weapons and implements of bronze"; so that it looks as if "the builders of the barrows were in the Bronze Age of civilization."[1] Still another band of the ancestors of the Japanese seems to have "completely emerged from the Bronze Age," and must have been in the Iron Age; for they buried their dead in dolmens, in which are found "weapons and implements of iron and vessels of wheel-turned pottery."[2]

This brings us to one more difficult subject for consideration in this chapter: Who were the ancestors of the Japanese; and were they the aborigines of Japan? The latter part of this double question should naturally be answered first. It now appears quite certain that the ancestors of the Japanese were not the aborigines of Japan; and some make a similar statement concerning the ancestors of the rapidly disappearing Ainu. The real aborigines are said to have been the aforementioned Koro-pok-guru, who were driven out by the Ainu into Sakhalin, the Kuriles, Kamchatka, and perhaps also to North America. But Dr. Munro is strongly of the opinion that these dwarfs never existed and that the Ainu were the aborigines of Japan.

The other part of the double question must receive a double answer. Even if we accept Brinkley's views of "three tides of more or less civilized immigrants," who settled respectively in Izumo, Yamato, and Kiūshiu, it looks as if the two latter may represent two movements of the same or closely related peoples. But there

---

[1] Brinkley, *Japan; Its History, Arts and Literature*, I, 41.

[2] *Ibid.*

are, and always have been, two very distinct types of Japanese; and these may be said, in a general way, to represent Mongol and Malay. The former, "neither Koreans nor Chinese," evidently reached Izumo via Korea; the latter naturally drifted up from the south on the Japan Current to Kiūshiu and to the Kii Promontory, in which is Yamato. These two types are still distinguishable physically: the patrician or aristocratic type is Mongoloid; while the plebeian type is Malayan. The latter "has a conspicuously dark skin, prominent cheek bones, a large mouth, a robust and heavily boned physique, a flat nose, full straight eyes, and a receding forehead." The former "is symmetrically and delicately built; his complexion varies from yellow to almost pure white; his eyes are narrow, set obliquely to the nose; the eyelids heavy; the eyebrows lofty; the mouth small; the face oval; the nose aquiline; the hand remarkably slender and supple."[1]

The band which made the political conquest of Japan and, with Jimmu, founded the one dynasty which has always ruled Japan, was probably Malayan.[2] But that conquest was quite like the Norman conquest of England, in that the victors became absorbed in the vanquished and the union produced a mighty nation.

---

[1] Brinkley, *Japan, Its History, Arts and Literature*, I, 35-40.

[2] For a discussion of "The Malay Element in Japan", see chap. ii of *The Japanese Nation in Evolution* (Griffis). In that book the author emphasizes his idea that the Original stock of the Japanese is Ainu. We are not yet convinced that he proves his point; we are inclined to think that he overestimates the Ainu element in Japanese civilization.

CHAPTER II. THE PREHISTORIC PERIOD

660 (?) B.C. - 400 (?) A.D.

We repeat here what we stated in the previous chapter, that, from the standpoint of the historical critic, this period and the preceding one might well be included together under the title of "Prehistoric." But, in view of the fact that the Japanese strictly mark off the "Divine Ages" (*Jindai*) as a period by itself, it has seemed best to follow that plan. Our second period, therefore, covers the time from the accession of Jimmu, when he set up his capital at Kashiwabara, until about 400 A.D. The date officially assigned to the former event is 660 B.C., from which the years of the Empire are reckoned, so that the year 1915 is the 2,575th year from the founding of the Empire. Even the day of Jimmu's accession is fixed (February 11), which is officially observed as a national holiday, under the name *Kigensetsu.*[1] And that was the day selected for the founding of a new empire by the promulgation of the constitution in 1889.

This "Prehistoric Period" is the one which is called by Peery that of "mythological history," and to which Griffis applies the expression "twilight of fable." What was said in the preceding chapter concerning the value of the traditions of the "Divine Ages" may be repeated here with more emphasis; for the myths and legends of the era under consideration have greater historical value than those of the preceding era, as we gradually approach nearer and nearer to historical records which can be more and more verified. It is impossible to mark out clearly just

---

[1] Another national holiday (April 3) is sacred to Jimmu. On the subject of Japanese chronology, consult *Transactions of the Asiatic Society of Japan*, Vol. XXXVII, Supplement, especially pp. i-x, 1-37, 257-61. Also see Murdoch, *History of Japan*, I, 75, 76.

where myth and legend cease and history begins, but it is quite interesting to observe how much more "historical" the narratives become toward the end of this period. At the beginning the mythological element is large and the historical is small; at the end of this period the mythological element has become small and the historical is large.

But, whether the date 660 B.C. can be accepted or not, it is interesting to make some comparison with synchronous periods in the history of other countries. It was the time when Assyria, under Sardanapalus, was at the height of its power; not long after the ten tribes of Israel had been carried into captivity, and soon after the reign of the good Hezekiah in Judah; before Media had risen into prominence; a century later than Lycurgus and a few decades before Draco; and during the Roman kingdom.

Concerning the eight emperors between Jimmu and Sujin, there is nothing of importance recorded in either the *Kojiki* or the *Nihongi,* which are filled up with uninteresting genealogies and other trifles. But during that interval the Empire seems to have extended its boundaries. According to one account[1] "the Emperor Jimmu's sway was limited to a few districts [nine provinces] in the neighborhood of Yamato," especially in what are now called the Five Home Provinces (around Kyōto); but "in the reign of Emperor Sujin the imperial authority had much wider bounds." During this reign, to which are assigned the years from 97 to 30 B.C., "generals were despatched in various directions and quickly subdued the designated provinces." "The five kinds of grain were produced and the peasantry enjoyed abundance." And in this reign, "taxes were for the first time levied on the proceeds of the chase and on the handiwork of women." In fact, this emperor was so popular that he received the title of "the first country-pacifying emperor." Indeed, we may

[1] *Official History of the Empire of Japan.*

say that Jimmu was the Cyrus, or founder, of the Japanese Empire, while Sujin, called "the Civilizer," was its Darius, or organizer.

The next emperor, Suinin, is credited with an incredible reign of about a century (29 B.C.-70 A.D.). But it was an important reign in regard to both internal and foreign affairs. "This sovereign also took measures to promote agriculture." It was during his reign that the "Three Insignia" (mirror, sword, and jewels), which had hitherto been kept in the palace and thus moved about as the location thereof changed, were deposited, in charge of an imperial princess, in the famous shrine of Ise. There the jewels and the mirror are still kept, while the sword now lies in the Atsuta Shrine. The present Ise Shrine is "an exact replica of that first erected more than nineteen hundred years ago by Yamato Hime (Princess), preserving all the primitive simplicity of construction without any outward adornment of color or carving, either in wood or in metal, of the architecture of the age in which she lived."[1] This shrine is rebuilt every twenty years.

The reign of Suinin was also marked by the first attempt to abolish the cruel custom of burying alive, with the dead, "retainers and horses that had been in their service," and whose agonizing cries could be heard night and day. It was suggested, just as in Rome, that "clay images of men and women and horses" be used instead. These have been found in burial mounds and mark the "birth of Japanese art." It is also said that Suinin dispatched to Korea some expedition called "the first ever sent by Japan to a foreign country."

Suinin's successor was Keikō, whose reign is dated from 71 to 130 A.D. He is much less famous than his son Yamato-Dake, who is represented as "pursuing a most daring and romantic career." And it has been truly said that "the myths concerning

---

[1] Longford, *Story of Old Japan*, p. 33.

him are among the most picturesque in Japanese history." Griffis calls him "the conqueror of the Kwantō," which was the large section of Japan of which Yedo was about the center. Yamato Dake had first the honor of subduing rebels in Kiūshiu, and was then sent on his more difficult, but also successful, task of bringing the barbarians of the northeastern districts into subjection. In Yedo Bay, his wife, Oto Tachibana-no-Hime, leaped into the raging waves as a sacrifice to the wrath of the sea-god, who then gave the hero safe passage across. His lament on Usui Pass for his lost wife (*Aa! tsuma!* – "Alas! [my] wife!") has given to art, history, and literature the well-known name Azuma.[1]

The fourteenth emperor, Chūai, reigned only eight years, when he died and was succeeded by his wife, known as Jingu, or Jingō. Her reign ran from 201 to 269 A.D., but is not generally included in the official records, where those years are added to the short reign of Chūai. The "semi-mythical" Empress Jingō[2] is most famous for her Jingoistic invasion of Korea early in the third century A.D. This expedition is a bone of contention among students of Japanese history. The native scholars are not inclined to be destructive in their criticisms. The German Hoffman thought that he might obtain "a sketch for the domain of history" by "stripping the native accounts of poetical and religious ornament." But Aston goes so far as to suggest that one might as well "attempt to extract a true narrative from the story of Cinderella by leaving out the mice, the pumpkin coach, and the fairy godmother!" And he states in another place that, "while there was an empress of Japan in the third century A.D., the statement that she conquered Korea is highly improbable."

There are many interesting features of the story, whether it is

---

[1] Griffis has an Interesting story of his career in chap. vii of *The Mikado's Empire*.

[2] Longford calls her "the greatest heroine in Japanese history."

historical or not. Favorable omens accompanied every step in the preparation and the prosecution of the enterprise. Two deities, one of gentle disposition to watch over the Empress, and one of warlike spirit to lead the squadron, accompanied the expedition. We are forcibly reminded of Vergil *Aeneid* when we read that "the wind-god sent a breeze; the sea-god raised the billows; all the great fishes of the ocean rose to the surface and encompassed the ships."

Brinkley makes an attempt to harmonize the difficulties concerning Jingō and her expedition to Korea in the following way:

> *Chinese annalists say, at the very time when Jingō's figure is so picturesquely painted on the pages of Japanese records, a female sovereign of Japan sent to the Court of China an embassy which had to beg permission from the ruler of northwestern Korea to pass through his territory en route westward. Thus, although the celebrated empress' foreign policy be stripped of its brilliant conquests and reduced to the dimensions of mere envoy-sending, her personality at least is recalled from the mythical regions.*[1]

This Japanese Amazon's son Ōjin (270-310 A.D.) demands a place in these records, not so much on account of his own achievements, but because he is the Japanese Mars, or Hachiman, whose shrines are still very numerous and popular. The Japanese records give the date 284 A.D. for the introduction of letters and the beginning of literature, when a celebrated scholar called Achiki visited Japan from Korea and was appointed tutor to the Emperor's son. He was followed by another scholar named Wani, under whose tuition the young

---

[1] *Japan; Its History, Arts and Literature,* I, 72, 73.

prince "acquired a thorough knowledge of the Chinese classics. This is the first recorded instance of the teaching of Chinese literature in Japan." But Aston is strongly of the opinion that a mistake of two sexagenary cycles, or 120 years, was made in the reckoning, and that these important events occurred about the beginning of the fifth century.[1]

One of the famous "characters" of this period is the Japanese Methuselah, Take-no-uchi, who is renowned for having lived to be over three hundred years old and for having served as Prime Minister to five emperors and one empress.

The successor of Ōjin was Nintoku (313-399 A.D.), who deserves special mention for his "beneficent sway," particularly shown in a well-known story, as follows: One day, having looked far and wide over the country from a lofty tower, he saw no smoke arising in the land, and from that inferred that the people were so poor that they were not cooking rice. Therefore he intermitted forced labor for three years, so that the people could raise rice. During that period the palace fell into ruin, so that "the wind and rain entered the chinks and soaked the coverlets." But when the emperor again looked forth from his tower he saw smoke arising plentifully and rejoiced in the people's prosperity, because "the people's poverty is no other than Our poverty; the people's prosperity is none other than Our prosperity."

At the close of the reign of Nintoku there is a great change in the character of the records. The incredibly long lives and reigns which had been a marked feature suddenly disappear and are succeeded by what we may almost call incredibly, or, at any rate, unusually, short reigns. The first seventeen rulers (counting Jingō separately) reigned 1,059 years (660 B.C.-399 A.D.), or more than 62 years on an average.[2] Or, if we omit Jingō from the

---

[1] *Transactions of the Asiatic Society of Japan*, XVI, 61-73.

[2] See "Chronological Table of Emperors and Empresses" in the Appendix.

count, we have sixteen rulers reigning, on an average, more than 66 years. But the next seventeen rulers reigned only 228 years (400-628 A.D.), or not quite 13½ years on an average. This is too significant to overlook, especially in view of the fact that about 400 A.D. official records began to be kept by historiographers. For that reason we end the era called the "Prehistoric Period" at 400 (?) A.D.

At this point, before we reach the period when foreign influences enter, we must make some reference, though necessarily brief, to the pure Japanese cult, Shintō. It can scarcely be called a "religion" in the strict sense of that term, but it may not unfairly be said that to some extent Shintō became "a system of patriotism exalted to the rank of a religion," i.e., it was a kind of ecclesiastical patriotism. Pure Shintō was a system in which the deification of forces of nature, family ancestors, local and national heroes, and emperors plays an important part. It had no dogmas, no sacred books (unless the *Kojiki* and the *Nihongi* may be so classed), "no philosophy, no code of ethics, no metaphysics." It summed up its theory of human duty in the following injunction: "Follow your natural impulses and obey the laws of the state." "Shintō is essentially a religion of gratitude and love."

One Shintō apologist asserted that "morals were invented by the Chinese because they were an immoral people; but in Japan there was no necessity for any system of morals, as every Japanese acted rightly if he only consulted his own heart"!

Shintō was, of course, polytheistic, but in general lacked idols, although the *gohei,* or paper fillets, some phallic and other figures, and the mirror seem to be emblems of deity and practically idols.

Another interesting feature of Shintō was the fact that the emperor, as in Rome, "was at the same time high priest (*pontifex maximus)* and king (*imperator)."* Moreover, a Shintō priest was a secular official.

Shintō required of its adherents nothing except worship at certain temples or shrines on stated days. A pure Shintō temple is an exceedingly plain affair, in front of which, at a little distance, is invariably set a *torii* or a series of *torii*. The form of ordinary worship was simple, as it consisted of washing the face, or hands, or both, in holy water; of ringing a bell, or clapping one's hands to attract the god's attention; of casting in a coin as an offering; of standing with clasped hands during a short prayer, and of making a farewell bow. Shintō prayers were for material, and not for moral and spiritual, blessings. Pilgrimages to holy spots, usually "high places," are important in Shintō.

Frequent lustrations were also required.

In 1872, the Department of Religion summed up the principles of Shintō in the following "commandments," which it then promulgated:

> *Thou shalt honor the gods and love thy country.*
> *Thou shalt clearly understand the principles of*
> *Heaven and the duty of man. Thou shalt revere the*
> *Mikado as thy sovereign, and obey the will of his*
> *court.*[1]

---

[1] *The Mikado's Empire*, p. 96. Limitation of space prevents further consideration of this interesting and important topic. It really needs more detailed and thorough study by means of such books as Griffls, *The Religions of Japan*; Lowell, *The Soul of the Far East and Occult Japan*; Knox, *The Development of Religion in Japan*; Hearn's various books; papers by Sir Ernest Satow and Dr. Fiorenz in the *Transactions of the Asiatic Society of Japan*, and Aston, *Shintō: The Way of the Gods*.

CHAPTER III. THE IMPERIALISTIC PERIOD

400 (?)- 794 A.D.

It is somewhere about the commencement of the fifth century that Japanese records begin to be kept officially, that Japanese chronicles begin to assume credibility, and that Japanese "history" really begins to be more or less reliable. Yet scholars are inclined to be skeptical also about the records of the fifth century.[1] And there is some reason for doubting the records of that period, because it "may justly be called the blackest era in the history of Japanese imperialism." Yōriaku (457-479 A.D.), on account of "wholesale slaughter" of members of the imperial family, has been called the "Nero of Japanese history."[2] Seinei (480-484) "carried out a similar massacre"; while Buretsu, or Muretsu (499-506), "ranks even below Yōriaku as a fierce and merciless despot."[3] It is, therefore, perhaps not strange that great families having administrative power "behaved with the utmost arrogance." Of these, the most prominent were the Mononobe and Soga families.

The predominance of certain families was largely due to the fact that the old patriarchal system of government prevailed. We must, however, be careful to interpret the word "family," not in the narrow sense in which it is commonly used in the Occident, but in the broader sense in which the word *familia* was used by the Romans. Naturally, therefore, in Old Japan, "the family which possessed the greatest number of kinsfolk possessed also

---

[1] The first date which can be verified by comparison with the annals of other countries, like China or Korea, is 461 A.D.

[2] To his reign is assigned the story of Urashima, the Japanese Rip Van Winkle.

[3] But Murdoch, in trying to find his way through the maze of this time, comes to the conclusion that Yōriaku and Buretsu may have been one and the same person.

the greatest power in the state." It was also true that, "as the Emperor held his power through his birth and the position of his family," in the same way "the most powerful families had hereditary rights to the highest offices."[1] This point must be kept in mind through the whole course of Japanese history.

About the middle of the sixth century Japan entered upon a new era, known as the Asuka Period[2] (550-700), which is the era of the introduction of Buddhism into Japan. It was in the year 552, during the reign of the Emperor Kimmei (540-571), that an envoy came from Kudara, one of the Korean provinces, with an image of Buddha and books explaining Buddhist doctrine. He also stated that all people from India to Korea were followers of Buddhism, which excelled all other religions. The Emperor is said to have remarked, upon hearing a brief explanation of this teaching: "Never from former days until now have we had the opportunity of listening to so wonderful a doctrine." He felt inclined to adopt the new faith; but, meeting opposition among his ministers, he gave the image to Soga, his prime minister, "with permission to worship it by way of trial." And when a pestilence visited the nation, it was not unnaturally considered a punishment for abandoning the Japanese Kami for the worship of a strange god. Soga, however, escaped the fate of Socrates for a similar offense. And, in the reign of Bidatsu (572-585), Buddhist books, images, image-makers, priests, and a nun were sent over from Korea; and in 587, during the short reign of Yōmei (586, 587), the Buddhist party at court triumphed.

Soon after this comes the red-letter reign of the Empress Suiko (593-628), with whose name and fame must be associated her nephew and prime minister, Umayado, best known by his posthumous title, Prince Shōtoku. This reign is marked by

---

[1] Saitō, *A History of Japan*.

[2] Named from a place near Nara.

several important matters.

In the first place, there was compiled in 620 a history, the *Kiōjiki*, "the first known work of this kind"; but it was unfortunately destroyed by fire.

In the second place, the zeal of both the Empress and Shōtoku in behalf of Buddhism was so great that the latter especially has been called "the founder of Japanese Buddhism." Murdoch calls him "the Constantine of Japanese Buddhism." According to Knox,[1] Buddhism "became the established religion" in 621 A.D.

In the third place, this was the time of the beginnings of Japanese painting. This art was borrowed from China; the first teachers were Buddhist priests from Korea in the sixth century; and the first school of painting in Japan is, therefore, called a Buddhist school. "The oldest picture in Japan of which there is any authentic record was painted, probably by a Korean priest in the beginning of the seventh century, on the plaster wall of the Buddhist temple Hōriōji at Nara."[2]

In the fourth place, according to Asakawa,[3] with the reign of Suiko began "the conscious adoption of Chinese political doctrines and institutions." This included, for instance, the lunar calendar (602), a code of court etiquette, the exchange of envoys, "the commencement of [formal] intercourse with China." And the most important manifestation of Chinese influence was seen in the "first written law[s]," Shōtoku *Seventeen-Article Constitution*, in accordance with which he organized the administration in such a way as to make it a real imperialism. And this was done, not so much by specific statutes, as by a series of "glittering generalities" of moral and political maxims.

---

[1] *The Development of Religion in Japan.*

[2] Dick, *Arts and Crafts of Old Japan.*

[3] *The Early Institutional Life of Japan.*

When Shōtoku, who had been made Prince Imperial, died, his loss was mourned by all the people. "They all said, 'The sun and moon have lost their brightness.'" Longford has well stated his achievements in the following words:

> *He left behind him peace where he had found strife*
> *and anarchy, the light of civilization in the place of*
> *the darkness of semi-barbarism, the knowledge and*
> *practice of art and science where there had been none*
> *before, reverential observance of a religion which was*
> *destined to mould the character of his countrymen*
> *for more than a thousand years.*[1]

And yet Shōtoku, like most reformers, did not live to see the full fruition of his hopes. This result was not realized till the Taikwa Reformation, which takes its name from the Taikwa[2] Era, which covered the first few years (645-649) of the reign of the Emperor Kōtoku (645-654). The name "Taikwa Reform[s]" belongs really to a series of changes extending over a period of more than half a century (645-700); but it is often, for convenience, called the "Reform of 645," and has been denominated "a great turning-point" in the history of Japan. Taken with the Restoration of 1868, "it forms one of the greatest crises of the national career of the Japanese people"; or, if the rise of Japanese feudalism is added, it is one of "three great historical incidents." This reform was, according to Asakawa, "Chinese in its organization of the state, and Japanese in its theory of sovereignty"; for the emperor became the actual ruler, so that this is the great "imperialistic" era.

Murdoch characterizes this reform as follows:

---

[1] Longford, *Story of Old Japan*, p. 70.

[2] The first Nengō, or year period. See Appendix for a complete table of these special eras.

*The Yamato sovereign was no longer to be merely the
head of the chief clan in Japan, with a feeble control
over the other great clan chieftains, and with no
direct control over the dependents of these.
Henceforth he was really to be the Emperor of Japan.
Every rood of the soil was theoretically supposed to
have been surrendered to him, – that is to say, the
theory of eminent domain was now effectually
established. The land thus surrendered was then
distributed to the subjects of the Emperor in
approximately equal portions. The holders of these
portions were subject to the national burden of
taxation.*[1]

The Emperors Tenchi (662-671) and Mommu (697- 707) were the most prominent among those who succeeded in asserting their actual sovereignty. They were also eminent for their services in the cause of education, as the former established the first school and the latter organized the first university. Murdoch calls Tenchi "one of the most enlightened sovereigns that ever sat upon the throne of Japan." He extended a welcome to large bodies of Korean immigrants. Although his predecessor, his own mother, died in 661, and he practically became emperor at once, he did not formally assume the title until 668, but carried on the administration as Prince Imperial. And he always "continued to live in a house built of trees with the bark on."

In Mommu's reign, moreover, occurs the first instance of cremation, and the "Taikwa Reform" culminated in the "Taihō[2] Statutes" which may be said to have codified the "laws" of Shōtoku. This code consisted of thirty chapters containing minute admonitions and prohibitions concerning all matters of

---

[1] *History of Japan*, I, 170, 171.

[2] From the Taiho Era (701-703).

civil law, and of twelve chapters of criminal statutes with penalties. The latter were five in number: capital punishment, exile, penal servitude, beating (with a stick), and scourging (with a whip). The regulations with reference to trade and commerce "suggest a well-ordered and strictly supervised system, but show also that officialdom usurped a right of arbitrary interference."[1]

The Emperor Mommu, dying at the early age of twenty-five, was succeeded by his mother, known as the Empress Gemmyō (708-715). Her reign is memorable because in 710 A.D. the capital was removed to Nara, where it remained for about seventy-five years. Nara was Japan's "first great city and her first permanent capital"; it was "laid out as a replica of the Chinese capital of Hsian." This period is therefore called the "Nara Epoch," when, as a poet has expressed it,

> Nara, the Imperial Capital,
> Blooms with prosperity,
> Even as the blossom blooms
> With rich color and sweet fragrance.

During this epoch political affairs were in some confusion, of which one illustration will suffice. The Empress Kōken, an ardent Buddhist, abdicated after a reign of eight years (749-757), and was succeeded by Prince Ōi, afterward known as the Emperor Junnin (758-764). The latter, however, owing to civil commotions, was dethroned and exiled to Awaji, and his mother again ascended the throne, but is known by another name, Shōtoku (765-770). "This was the first instance of an emperor being exiled," and "posterity gave to the sovereign thus unfortunately distinguished the name of the 'Dethroned Emperor of Awaji.'" And at this time a Buddhist monk, Dōkyō, was "the most powerful subject in the Empire – head of the

---

[1] Brinkley, *Japan; Its History, Arts and Literature*, VI, 127.

church, spiritual director and chief physician to the Empress." He was even taken into the palace by his imperial mistress and given a kind of imperial title *(Hō-ō)*. And it is said that, "incredible as it may sound, the monk was aiming at nothing less than supplanting the line of the sun-goddess on the imperial throne of Japan."[1]

The Nara Epoch was pre-eminently a "woman's era." It is generally taken to cover, not merely the three-quarters of a century during which the capital was actually located at Nara, but also the few years following until the capital was located at Kyōto. The eight reigns of this period (710-794) include four by emperors and four by empresses. And altogether there have been only ten empresses besides Jingō.

The Nara Epoch was also a period of literary and aesthetic activity. In 712, in the reign of an empress, the *Kojiki* was completed; and in 720, in the reign of another empress, the *Nihongi* was finished. This is the period which Aston calls "the Golden Age of poetry," as especially illustrated by the *Manyōshiu,* or "Collection of Myriad Leaves." They numbered more than 4,000 pieces, chiefly *tanka,* or short poems of thirty-one syllables, but also including *naga-uta,* or long poems. Many of the authors of this period were women. The two most prominent poets represented in the *Manyōshiu* were Hitomaro and Akahito.

Aesthetic activity was manifested particularly in sculpture and metal work. It was the time of Gyōgi, "who ranks among Japan's greatest sculptors," and of the Dai Butsu, or Great Buddha, of Nara. This is 53 feet in height, and "is the greatest bronze statue that has ever been cast." It was also the time of the casting of the great bell in the temple known as Tōdaiji in Nara: this bell is 13 feet 6 inches high, with a diameter across the rim of 9 feet 1 inch, and it weighs over 40 tons. And the

---

[1] Murdoch, *History of Japan,* I, 199.

aforementioned temple, containing both the statue and the bell, itself dates back to the eighth century and is "yet almost as perfect as when first built."

The art of this period is thought to have been to some extent the indirect result of a "wave of Greek feeling," which had "produced in India a kind of Greco-Buddhist art." This came to Japan through Central Asia, China, and Korea, whence at this period came "letters, religion, philosophy, literature, law, ethics, medicine, science, and art," "the most potent factors in any civilization." In the famous temple Hōriōji, near Nara, scholars find Indian, Chinese, and Greek styles of architecture. "The pillars of the outer gate are partly Doric; other parts, for example, the roof, the windows, and the galleries, are Chinese, while the interior is Indian." And Dillon[1] says, of the art of the Nara Period, that "nothing is more remarkable than the undoubted presence of Persian, more precisely of Sassanian, motives in a considerable number of cases." In another place he alludes to "Indian or Saracenic" motives "in the symmetrical patterns."

From what has already been written, it is quite evident that this was a period of strong Buddhist influence in all lines of civilization. It is true that Confucianism had also entered Japan (in the sixth century); but "it remained practically stationary for a thousand years," and Buddhism was "the dominant force in the thoughts of Japan."

This was the period of the origin and development of the first six sects of Japanese Buddhism, of which Nara was the "center of propagation." These ancient sects are the Kusha, the Jōjitsu, the Ritsu, the Hossō, the Sanron, and the Kegon, of which all except the last one have become extinct. The earliest of these were the Jōjitsu and the Sanron, followed by the Hossō and the Kusha, all

---

[1] *The Arts of Japan.*

in the seventh century; while the Kegon and the Ritsu sects date from the eighth century. The Kusha, the Jōjitsu, and the Ritsu sects belong to the school known as *Hinayana,* or Smaller Vehicle; the Hossō and the Sanron sects to that known as the Middle Path *(Madhiyamika);* and the Kegon sect to that called *Mahayana,* or Greater Vehicle.

The Kusha sect taught "control of the passions and the government of thought," and "the burden of its philosophy is materialism." The Jōjitsu teaching was "pure nihilism, or the non-existence of both self and matter." The Ritsu sect "occupied itself exclusively with the higher ethics, the higher meditations, and the higher knowledge" and "exerted a powerful influence on the court" at Nara, which was made "beautiful to the eyes of faith as well as of sight." The Hossō doctrine was "subjective idealism," including "complete indifference to mundane affairs," because "thought only is real."

The Sanron Shō, or Three Shastra sect, allowed "greater breadth of view and catholicity of opinion"; but "the burden of this sect's teaching is infinite negation or absolute nihilism." In the teaching of the Kegon sect "matter and thought are one" and its doctrine was "the unconditioned or realistic pantheism."[1]

And even in this early period of the history of Buddhism in Japan we begin to find evidence of the truth of the statement that "Buddhism is essentially a religion of compromise." About the middle of the eighth century, when Japan was visited by famine and pestilence, the Shintō disciples laid the calamities at the door of the "strange faith." But "the great Buddhist priest Gyōgi saved the situation by a singularly clever theory. He taught that the sun-goddess... had been merely an incarnation of the Buddha,

---

[1] These summaries are from Griffis, *The Religions of Japan.* See also Nanjō, *Short History of the Japanese Buddhist Sects*, and papers by Lloyd and Anesaki in the *Transactions of the Asiatic Society of Japan.*

and that the same was true of all the members of the Shintō pantheon." And it was to celebrate this reconciliation of Shintō and Buddhism that the Dai Butsu was set up at Nara; "the copper used for the body of the image representing the Shintō faith, the gold that covered it typifying Buddhism."[1] This theory was afterward organized into what was known as Ryōbu Shintō, of which more later.

To summarize the influence of Buddhism upon Japanese civilization there is nothing better than Chamberlain's words:

> All education was for centuries in Buddhist hands, as
> was the care of the poor and sick; Buddhism
> introduced art, introduced medicine, moulded the
> folk-lore of the country, created its dramatic poetry,
> deeply influenced politics and every sphere of social
> and intellectual activity. In a word, Buddhism was
> the teacher under whose instruction the Japanese
> nation grew up.[2]

One way in which Buddhist influence was soon felt in political affairs was by encouraging the practice of abdication, so that the emperors and empresses might retire to a life of seclusion and meditation in monastery or convent. And this led gradually to great abuses. Energetic individuals of a noble family, in that way, got the administration into their own hands. As early as the middle of the seventh century (645) the Fujiwara family commenced to monopolize the civil offices and to supply wives or concubines to the degenerate emperors. This kind of "supervising statesmanship" they continued, with more or less success, for four or five centuries. And during the greater part of that period they were the practical rulers of the Empire, so that it is about time to bring to a close this era specially denominated

---

[1] Brinkley, *Japan; Its History, Arts and Literature*, I, 96.

[2] *Things Japanese.*

"imperialistic." And there is no more convenient date than 794 A.D., when the Emperor Kwammu (782-805) located his capital at a place known as Uda, renamed Heian-kyō, or "Capital of Peace," but best known as Miyako or Kyōto.

CHAPTER IV. THE HEIAN EPOCH

794-1159 A.D.

This period might be entitled "Fujiwara Bureaucracy." As was stated at the close of the preceding chapter, the Fujiwara family began as early as 645 A.D. to monopolize the civil offices and to control the imperial Court by a kind of "supervising statesmanship." It was perhaps the first case of a political "ring" in Japanese history. "Every new office, as fast as created, was filled by them." It is true that it was not till the latter part of the ninth century that the titles of Sesshō and Kwampaku,[1] both of which seem to correspond to "regent," were conferred on Fujiwara statesmen, and thus "the imperial authority passed virtually into the hands of the Fujiwara family." But, as the substance is more than the title, it is not out of place to make the Heian and Fujiwara epochs practically synchronous.

It is well also to notice a point made by Hearn, that "the remarkable duration of the Fujiwara rule, as compared with others, may perhaps be accounted for by the fact that the Fujiwara represented a religious, rather than a military, aristocracy."[2] He asserts that "the Fujiwara were a religious aristocracy, claiming divine origin – clan-chiefs of a society in which religion and government were identical, and holding to that society much the same relation as the Eupatridae to the ancient Attic society." Nor should the fact be ignored that the Fujiwara Bureaucracy was maintained by constant resort to the encouragement of abdication on the part of the emperors, and to setting upon the throne in their places youths or mere children, who would, of course, need the supervision of a Fujiwara. The

---

[1] Brinkley translates the latter, "Lord Chancellor."

[2] *Japan : An Interpretation*, pp. 307, 289.

latter, however, were very careful to maintain "the center of political gravity" in the Court; to base their own power "on matrimonial alliances with the throne"; and to govern "through the Emperor." But, none the less, they became "the proprietors of the throne and dictated as to who should be made Emperor." And Seiwa (859-876) enjoyed the double honor of being not only the first child emperor, but also the first male sovereign to reign under a regent. And that was the first time that "the great office of Regent was filled, not by an august descendant of the sun-goddess but by a mere subject," of the Fujiwara family. In fact, during the Fujiwara Bureaucracy it was only the children of Fujiwara consorts of the emperors who "could hope to be placed on the throne."[1]

The Heian Epoch is taken to begin when the Emperor Kwammu (782-805) located his capital at Uda, now known as Kyōto. This event was a "subject of national rejoicing," so that the people gave to the place a new name, Heian-kyō, or "Capital of Peace." But the era was far from one of tranquillity, as will be very evident as we proceed. The new capital was laid out quite regularly and with much grandeur. "The streets lay parallel and at right angles, like the lines on a checkerboard"; and "an elaborate system of subdivision was adopted."[2] The imperial citadel and palace were located in the center of the northern section of the city.

It was in the reign of Kwammu that the posthumous names now used for all the emperors, from Jimmu down to Kwammu's predecessor, were selected by a famous scholar. Toward the end of the eighth century the renowned general, Tamura-maro, at the head of an expedition again the rebellious Ainu in the northern province of Mutsu, succeeded in completely

---

[1] Murdoch, *History of Japan*, I, 238, 239.
[2] See *Official History*, pp. 104, 105.

subjugating them.[1] It is claimed by Brinkley that Kwammu "ranks as one of Japan's three greatest sovereigns – Tenchi, Kwammu, and Go-Daigo (Daigo II)," because "he essayed to get into close touch with the people." Kwammu was a "schoolmaster emperor," because he had been serving as rector of the university; and he is reckoned by Murdoch among the very few Japanese emperors "who have proved themselves to be statesmen."[2] For he not only reigned but also ruled. And Brinkley thinks that Kwammu's reign "marks the parting of the ways in mediaeval Japan"; for "his was the last really resolute struggle made during three and a half centuries to stem the influences that were plainly tending toward the substitution of bureaucracy for imperialism, the subordination of the throne to the nobility."

But there were rival families to dispute the supremacy of the Fujiwara. One of the most prominent of these was the Sugawara family, of whom the best-known representative is Michizane. This was a literary family; and Michizane was "a brilliant scholar in Chinese." He was the tutor of the Emperor Uda (888-896), and became a counsellor and minister of Uda's son and successor, Daigo (897-930). But the Fujiwara regent finally succeeded in having this "wise and honest counsellor" transferred, by a kind of "honorable banishment," to a position in the island of Kiōshiu, where he soon died. But the famous scholar has since been deified under the name of Tenjin, and is "the patron saint of men of letters and of students."

The period of Daigo's rule is regarded by some as "the Golden Age of Japanese history" because "his administration was based on care for the people." But it was only a few years later

---

[1] He is also said to have been the first person to bear the title *Sei-i-Tai Shōgun* ("Subduing-Barbarian-Great-General"), which later became so important.

[2] The others whom he includes in this category are Tenchi and the late Emperor Meiji. In another place he includes Go-Sanjō, or Sanjō II.

that the "only instance of a rebellion directed against the throne" occurred. Taira Masakado, Governor of the provinces of Kazusa, Shimōsa, and Hitachi, raised the standard of rebellion and proclaimed himself Emperor.[1] And in the province of Iyo, Fujiwara Sumitomo also led a revolt against the government. The latter, however, succeeded in defeating and beheading these rebels. But, as Masakado's ghost used to haunt the earth, the rebel was apotheosized in the thirteenth century and is still one of the deities worshiped at the shrine of Kanda Myōjin behind the Educational Museum in Hongō Ward, Tōkyō.

For about half a century nothing happened worth chronicling. The Emperor Ichijō, whose reign (986-1011) covered the change from the tenth to the eleventh century, was a well-educated man, whose reign "was marked by the works of several savants," including learned women.

It was only a few years later, during the reign of Go-Ichijō (Ichijō II) (1016-1036), when "the power and influence of the Fujiwara reached their zenith." The most powerful chief of that clan was Michinaga, who died in 1027. It is said that he "once composed a stanza, the purport of which was that all the world seemed to have been created for his uses, and that every desire he felt was satisfied as completely as the full moon is perfectly rounded." The condition of this time is described in a work appropriately called *Eigwa Monogatari,* or "Story of Grandeur."

About fifty years later the Emperor Shirakawa seems to have succeeded in curbing temporarily the power of the Fujiwara and to have been the actual ruler of the country, not only during his own nominal reign (1073-1086), but also for more than forty years after he had abdicated and taken the title of *Hō-ō.*[2] But, in

---

[1] He seems to have arranged with some man to go about shouting, "I am the messenger of Hachiman Bosatsu, who bestows the Imperial dignity upon his descendant, Taira Masakado."

[2] This word is now used for the pope; then it meant "cloistered emperor."

this way, he "himself inaugurated a new form of the very abuse he had abolished: he instituted a system of *camera* emperors... He virtually directed affairs of state... The reigning sovereign had only to fold his hands and follow the counsels of his predecessor." This rule of Shirakawa extended over the reigns of three nominal sovereigns, until his death in 1129. Even when he was "cloistered Emperor," "he maintained a Court of his own, with officials and guards and all the state that surrounded the actual occupant of the throne."

Shirakawa, however, seems to have been so largely under the influence of the Buddhist priesthood that he was unable to restrain their lawlessness when they began to employ "sacerdotal soldiers," trained in "barrack monasteries," to enforce their demands. Indeed, Shirakawa is the one who gave utterance to the following well-known lament: "There are but three things in my dominions that do not obey me: the waters of the Kamo River, the dice of *Sugoroku* [backgammon] players, and the priests of Buddha."

These great monasteries had long been amassing wealth and power and had found it necessary to hire mercenaries for protection against attacks from rivals and for aggressive measures. "Each of them had become a huge Cave of Adullam – a refuge for every sturdy knave with a soul above earning a livelihood by the commonplace drudgery of honest work. Each of them had in truth assumed the aspect of a great fortress."[1]

During the reign of Shirakawa's son, Horikawa (1087- 1106), there arose another disturbance in Northern Japan, where the population consisted largely of Ainu and adventurous Japanese. A Minamoto chief, named Yoshiiye, was sent against the rebels and, though it took him years to bring them into subjection, he acquired so much fame by this campaign that he became known

---

[1] Murdoch, *History of Japan*, I, 290, 291.

as Hachiman Tarō, and thus ranked as the eldest son of the war god. He was also "the first archer of national renown"; and Tametomo, one of his descendants, was the most famous Japanese archer, of whose strength and skill many marvelous tales are related. One of these stories is a variant of the tale about William Tell and the apple; and another relates a Samsonic exploit when Tametomo's arm healed after the muscles had been cut. He is said after that to have escaped to the Riūkiū Islands and to have founded the dynasty of kings who ruled over those islands.

The references in this chapter to Taira and Minamoto hint that the end of the Fujiwara Bureaucracy and of the Heian Epoch is drawing near. The Emperor Shirakawa did what has often been done elsewhere. Just as Vortigern, the British king of Kent, is said to have invited the Jute leaders, Hengist and Horsa, to protect his realm against the incursions of the Picts, so Shirakawa begged the military families of the Taira and the Minamoto to come to the capital (Kyōto) to protect it from the priests. The usual result followed in this case. In 1155 A.D. the Emperor Shirakawa II ascended the throne, but was attacked by an ex-emperor, Sutoku, who wished to resume the imperial power. In this strife the Minamoto family was divided, but the Taira family espoused the cause of the new emperor and was successful. Shirakawa II, however, soon abdicated and was succeeded by his son, Nijō (1159-1164). Strife then arose between Minamoto Yoshitomo and Taira Kiyomori, the latter of whom was victorious. In these two contests the Fujiwara family was completely ruined; so that, with the victory of Kiyomori in 1159 A.D. may end both the Fujiwara Bureaucracy and the Heian Epoch. Henceforth, for a long period of several centuries, "Japan was governed not by the scepter, but by the sword." The Japanese Jutes, Angles, and Saxons (the Taira and the Minamoto) dispossessed the Japanese Britons (the Fujiwara).

While the Heian Epoch was far from such a period as its name might indicate, it is yet interesting for its developments in the peaceful pursuits of civilization. It was during this era that two powerful Buddhist sects, the Tendai and the Shingon, were founded, the former by Saichō and the latter by Kukai. The chief temple of the former was established on Mount Hiei, northeast of Kyōto; that of the latter on Mount Kōya in Yamato. Both of these sects belong to what is known as the Great[er] Vehicle (*Mahayana*). The Tendai doctrines are based on "pantheistic realism" and recognize a large number of deities, whose idols are worshiped. The Shingon ("True Word") sect taught "three great secret laws, regarding Body, Speech, and Thought"; its philosophy includes mysticism and pantheism. The Tendai teachers were ascetics and have also been called "the Jesuits of Japan"; the Shingon believers seem to be "Buddhist Gnostics."

The most interesting feature of the Buddhism of this epoch was the wholesale adoption of Shintō deities into the pantheon as incarnations of Buddha. This idea was formulated by Kukai, or Kōbō Daishi (774-835), into a regular system, afterward known as Ryōbu Shintō, which was maintained for more than a millennium. Concerning this composite religion, which illustrates the Japanese facility for compromise, Knox says that, "while the name was Shintō, the substance was Buddhism."

The genius of Kōbō Daishi was further manifested, if we may trust tradition, in the invention of the Japanese *hira-gana,* or running script, which consists of forty-seven cursive forms of entire Chinese characters. The *kata-kana,* or side script, consisting of sides or parts of Chinese characters, is accredited to a man named Kibi-no Mabi, who died in 776 A.D.[1] The latter are

---

[1] He is also credited with having brought from China the game of *go* (slightly resembling, but much more complicated than, the Occidental checkers), the knowledge of the art of embroidery, and the *biwa,* or four stringed lute.

arranged in a partly artificial table of fifty sounds *(gojiu-on)*. The former were arranged by Kabō Daishi in an artificial poem, which reads as follows:

> *Iro wa nioedo*
> *Chirinuru wo –*
> *Waga yo tare zo*
> *Tsune naran?*
> *Ui no oku-yama*
> *Kyō koete,*
> *Asaki yume miji,*
> *Ei mo sezu.*

Professor Chamberlain's revised translation is the following:

> *Though gay in hue, [the blossoms] flutter down alas!*
> *Who, then, in this world of ours, may continue*
> *forever? Crossing today the uttermost limits of*
> *phenomenal existence, I shall see no more fleeting*
> *dreams, neither be any longer intoxicated.*

In brief, "All is vanity."

The religious spirit of this epoch affected its artistic works, which "are full of intense fervor and nearness to the gods." Kanaoka, however, was also "the first great secular painter of Japan," and was "especially famous as a painter of horses." It is also interesting to note that it is considered "possible that the beginnings of Japanese art were strongly affected by Persian influences," which are thought to be discernible in Kanaoka's pictures. In the tenth century was founded "the first purely native school, called the Yamato School, which afterward, under the name of the Tosa School, became the recognized style for the treating of historical subjects." It was the beginning of "a new development in Japanese art and culture, which may be termed the *national,* in contrast to the predominating *continental* ideas of preceding epochs."[1] The Heian Epoch is the Classical Period, the Elizabethan Era, and the Woman's Era of Japanese literature. Its anthology includes the poetry of the *Kokinshiu,* the sketches of *Makura-no-Sōshi,* the diary known as *Tosa Nikki,* and *Genji Monogatari* in fiction. The most famous poets represented in the *Kokinshiu* are Yukihira, Narihira, Tsurayuki, and Ono-no-Komachi, "the great sad poetess whose life exemplifies the loves and sorrows of that refined and voluptuous epoch." The *Tosa Nikki,* or Tosa Diary, describes a trip made by the author, Tsurayuki, from Tosa to Kyōto, and is said to be the "best extant embodiment of uncontaminated Japanese speech." It has been translated into English by the late Mrs. Flora Best Harris with the title *Log of a Japanese Journey. Makura-no Sōshi,* or "Pillow Sketches," by a woman named Sei Shonagon, is called "one of the most polished literary sketches ever produced in Japan, as the *Genji-Monogatari* was a peerless novel." The author of the latter was also a woman, named Murasaki no Shikibu, whom Aston compares with both Fielding and Richardson as a realistic novelist. And Aston says that these last two works "by common consent mark the highest point to which the classical literature of Japan attained."[2] By these four literary classics, the first two of the tenth century and the last two of the eleventh century, rather than by political intrigues or nascent art or even Buddhist activity, we should remember the Heian Epoch.

---

[1] See Dillon, *The Arts of Japan,* and Dick, *Arts and Crafts of Old Japan.*

[2] See Aston, *History of Japanese Literature.*

CHAPTER V. THE GEMPEI ERA

1159-1199 A.D.

The name of this era is a compound of Gen, meaning Minamoto, and Hei, meaning Taira. The former of these clans was known by its white flags and the latter by its red flags; so that one is naturally reminded of the Wars of the Roses in England. Unfortunately, in Japan there was no Henry of Lancaster or Elizabeth of York by whose marriage to unite the warring clans.

This period is a very short one, but its four decades include events of intense interest. And this brief era must be subdivided into two periods: one that of Taira Supremacy (1159-1185), and the other that of Minamoto Supremacy (1185-1199). This is, moreover, the beginning of military domination and the conclusion of civil imperialism, which thereafter generally existed only in name until the Restoration of 1868. But the usurpations of the Taira, the Minamoto, and later of the Tokugawa differed from that of the Fujiwara, described in the preceding chapter, in that these families based their power "on the possession of armed strength which the throne had no competence to control"; governed "in spite of the Emperor"; and "transferred the center of political gravity to a point altogether outside the Court, the headquarters of a military feudalism."[1]

a) *Taira supremacy* (1159-1185). – When Taira Kiyomori quelled the Heiji disturbance,[2] it was truly the end of the Fujiwara supremacy and seemed to be also the complete ruin of the Minamoto clan. Their chief representative, Yoritomo, was sent into exile in Izu, where, being a mere boy, he was supposed to be not at all dangerous. He had a younger half-brother,

---

[1] Brinkley, *Japan; Its History, Arts and Literature*, I, 158, 159.

[2] Heiji was the name of the year 1159.

Yoshitsune, whose life was also spared by Kiyomori on condition that his mother, the well-known Tokiwa, "a peasant girl of surpassing beauty," become the victor's concubine. Thus, in spite of the remonstrances of Kiyomori's retainers, the Taira leader allowed love to triumph over prudence and spared those who were destined to annihilate the Taira clan. In such a way are the revenges of history often accomplished.

Meanwhile Kiyomori rose in power and authority until in 1167 he became Prime Minister *(Dajō Daijin)*, and "was thus virtually the ruler of Japan." And "this was, in truth, the first instance of a military noble's participation in the administration of state affairs, and it may be regarded as the dawn of an era when they were to fall entirely under military control." Kiyomori followed the example of the Fujiwara clan in the practice of nepotism by filling the "prominent positions in the central and local governments" with his kinsmen and followers, and in marrying his daughter to the Emperor Takakura (1168-1180), who began to reign at the age of eight. And when we notice that several emperors ascended the throne as young as six, four, three, and even one, it is not difficult to understand how the Taira clan maintained its supremacy in the administration of affairs.

Moreover, according to Saitō,[1] "half of the whole of the Japanese Empire was in the private ownership of the Taira family. It was said at that time that no one who did not belong to the race of the Taira was a man. The family soon became so arrogant and proud that it was universally hated."

But the day of reckoning was at hand, for Yoritomo and Yoshitsune had been growing up and preparing for revenge. The latter had been intended for a priest, but he "refused to have his head shaved off, and in the monastery was irrepressibly merry,

---

[1] *A History of Japan.*

lively, and self-willed." He was nicknamed Ushiwaka, or Young Ox, by the monks, to whom he gave great trouble and even "scandalized their reverences." Finally, "chafing at his dull life," he managed to escape, to the relief of the priests, to Mutsu, in Northern Japan, where he spent his time in military exercises. "At the age of twenty-one he had won a reputation as a soldier of peerless valor and consummate skill, and the exponent of the loftiest code of Japanese chivalry." He was truly the Bayard of Japan. Yoritomo, too, had been preparing for the part he was to play, not only by martial discipline, but also by marrying Masago, daughter of Hōjō Tokimasa, "an able man, in whose veins ran imperial blood."

The contest began in 1180, the year when Kiyomori fixed his headquarters at Kamakura. In 1181 Kiyomori died, at the age of sixty-four, with the following farewell message:

> *My regret is only that I am dying and have not yet*
> *seen the head of Yoritomo of the Minamoto. After*
> *my decease, do not make offerings to Buddha on my*
> *behalf nor read sacred books. Only cut off the head of*
> *Yoritomo of the Minamoto and hang it on my tomb.*
> *Let all my sons and grandsons, retainers and*
> *servants, each and every one, follow out my*
> *commands, and on no account neglect them.*[1]

This dying wish was never to be fulfilled: and after Kiyomori's death the struggle became fiercer. In 1184, Yoritomo's cousin, Yoshinaka, led the Minamoto forces to Kyōto, which fell into their hands. The Taira, with the young Emperor Antoku (1180-1185) and the Sacred Sword and Seal, fled to Sanuki in the island of Shikoku and established the Court there. Consequently the Minamoto clan set up Antoku's younger

---

[1] Griffis, *The Mikado's Empire*, p. 133.

brother as Emperor (Toba II, or Go-Toba)." This was the first coronation ceremony ever conducted without due transfer of the Three Sacred Insignia to the new monarch."

Yoshinaka, known as *Asahi-Shogun* ("Morning-Sun General") "on account of the suddenness and brilliancy of his rising," and intoxicated by his success, had himself appointed *Sei-i-Shōgun* ("Subduing-Barbarian-General"). But Yoritomo dispatched against him Yoshitsune, who so severely defeated him that he committed suicide.

Yoshitsune then pushed on over into Shikoku and drove the Taira forces with the Emperor out of Sanuki, whence they fled in junks. The decisive contest was the famous naval battle of Danno-ura (1185), in which the Minamoto won a complete victory after "a terrible hand-to-hand fight."[1] When the Emperor's grandmother saw that escape was no longer possible, she took the young boy, with the Sword and the Seal, in her arms and jumped into the sea. The Sword was lost, but the Seal was afterward recovered. Only a small remnant of the Taira survived this battle and fled to the mountains of Higo. Many of the women who survived had to support themselves by becoming courtesans in Shimonoseki, where, to its shame be it written, occurs a periodical procession of courtesans to the shrine of their patron saint, the young Antoku. And the ghosts of the dead Taira have ever since haunted that dreadful spot. "Even today the Chōshiu peasant fancies he sees the ghostly armies baling out the sea with bottomless dippers, condemned thus to cleanse the ocean of the stain of centuries ago."[2] And the influence of this awful slaughter may be seen also on the crabs, which are known as the Heike crabs, because the stern face of a Taira warrior is stamped upon their shells.

---

[1] Murdoch thinks that Yoshitsune's military genius was Napoleonic.

[2] Griffis, *Japan in History, Folk-Lore and Art.*

b) *Minamoto supremacy* (1185-1199). – With this practical annihilation of the Taira clan, the Minamoto clan obtained supremacy and effected "the complete establishment of military feudalism in Japan." This was accomplished by Yoritomo, whom Brinkley calls "the most remarkable figure during the first eighteen centuries of Japanese history." The changes which he made were "radical," and they "signified a complete shifting of the center of power" from the south to the north – to Kamakura, concerning which Yoritomo might well have quoted Nebuchadnezzar's boast: "Is not this great Babylon, which I have built... by the might of my power and for the glory of my majesty?" Yoritomo's success is regarded by Brinkley as a "revolution in a double sense," because it was not only the substitution of a military democracy for an imperial aristocracy, but also the rehabilitation of a large section of the nation who had once been serfs "of Kyōto nobles."[1]

Murdoch emphasizes Yoritomo's original and constructive statesmanship in the following terms:

> *While making himself Mayor of the Palace, he studiously kept at a distance of more than three hundred miles – a journey of four days for a swift courier – from the Court and its frivolities, and while professing to restore those old institutions of Japan which had hopelessly outlived their usefulness, he supplemented them by institutions which were so vitally necessary to the changed and changing spirit of the times that they insensibly supplanted them.*[2]

Saitō notes that

> *the foundation of the Shōgunate was not a mere*

---

[1] Brinkley, *Japan; Its History, Arts and Literature*, Vol. II.

[2] *A History of Japan*, I, 372, 373.

> *chance or passing event in the historical development*
> *of Japan, nor must it be regarded merely as the act of*
> *any one great man like Yoritomo. It was the result of*
> *a long evolution which marks the essential character*
> *of the Japanese Empire, the evolution of the feudal*
> *system which had its beginnings in the time of the*
> *Fujiwara.*

One terrible blot on Yoritomo's character was his treatment of Yoshitsune, to whom he was chiefly indebted for his final victory over the Taira. "Jealousy, envy, suspicion, and cold-heartedness were the great moral weaknesses of Yoritomo." Impelled by jealousy and false accusations, he refused to permit Yoshitsune to enter Kamakura. Although the latter sent to his elder brother a letter – "one of the most pathetic documents in Japanese literature" – to plead his cause and to ask merely for justice, the appeal was in vain. Later, it was determined that Yoshitsune must be "removed." The story of the manner in which Yoshitsune and his *fidus Achates,* Benkei, eluded Yoritomo, is a classic. But the young hero finally committed suicide *(harakiri).* Some, however, claim that he escaped and lived among the Ainu, who even now have a shrine to his honor at Piratori in the Hokkaidō. Others, moreover, have identified him with Genghis Khan!

In 1192, Yoritomo became *Sei-i-Tai-Shōgun.* That title had heretofore been conferred only for limited special purposes; but now the authority of the office was general: "to provide for the defense and tranquillity of the Empire at large." And it also "put the whole military class and the whole military resources of the Empire at his [Yoritomo's] disposal" in case of need. Yoritomo did not long enjoy this authority, but died in 1199, when the real power passed into the hands of his wife's family, the Hōjō. He, however, deserves honor for the great "administrative machine" which he created.

Since this period was so brief and largely occupied with warfare, it is not strange that it produced no art or literature worthy of mention. But it was a period of such stirring adventures as to furnish subjects for men of later days. The mighty Yoritomo, the beautiful Tokiwa, the chivalrous Yoshitsune and Benkei, and others are the heroes and the heroines of many works of art and of literary productions like *Gempei Seisuiki, Heiji Monogatari, Hōgen Monogatari,* and *Heike Monogatari.* And Longford points out an interesting coincidence: "While Yoshitsune and Benkei were wandering amidst the maples of Yoshino, Richard Cœur de Lion and Robin Hood were simultaneously holding revel amidst the oaks of Sherwood, and what the latter are in English history, Yoshitsune and Benkei are in that of Japan."[1]

---

[1] *Story of Old Japan*, p. 130.

CHAPTER VI. HŌJŌ TYRANNY

1199-1333 A.D.

The word "tyranny" is used here, not only in the modern, but also in the ancient, sense, and refers, therefore, not merely to arbitrary exercise of power, of which there were plenty of instances during this period, but also to the illegal assumption of authority. Indeed, this era might be named "Hōjō Usurpation." It will be remembered that Yoritomo obtained for a wife Masago, the capable daughter of a noble named Hōjō. When Yoritomo died, the truth was evident of that Japanese proverb, *Taishō ni tane ga nashi,* or, "To a general there is no seed"; for, although he had children, there was no worthy heir. His son Yoriiye nominally succeeded as Shōgun; but he preferred "a life of pleasure and gayety" to the onerous duties of government. Therefore the administration of affairs naturally fell into the hands of his maternal grandfather, Hōjō Tokimasa. Later there was established in connection with the Shōgunate at Kamakura the office of Regent *(Shikken),* or Vice-Regent, by whom the Empire was governed through a puppet Shōgun of a puppet Emperor. This state of affairs continued for one and a third centuries, and was generally marked by cruelty and rapacity. "The Hōjō have never been forgiven for their arbitrary treatment of the Mikados... To this day, historian, dramatist, novelist, and storyteller delight to load. them with vilest obloquy... The country folks of eastern Japan have a great annual ceremony for the extermination of a destructive worm called the 'Hōjō bug.' "[1]

This era is also called the Kamakura Period, because that place, founded by Yoritomo, became a second capital and the

---

[1] Griffls, *The Mikado's Empire,* p. 157. See also Murdoch, *History of Japan,* I, chap. xv.

first center of influence. This is the name given to the period in Japanese literature; and the subtitle, "Decline of Learning," characterizes the era. We may therefore dismiss the literature with the statement that the only great work, but that a real classic, is the *Hōjōki,* by Chōmei, who has been called "the Japanese Wordsworth," but is more nearly "the Japanese Thoreau." The resemblance of the name of this little book to that of the period is only apparent. *Hōjō* means "ten feet square" and indicates the size of the hut in which Chōmei lived his hermit life; and *ki* means "record." The book was written in 1212.[1]

Within a few years after Yoritomo's death several changes had taken place in the personnel of the administration. In 1203 his son Yoriiye was deposed in favor of his brother Sanetomo, and was murdered the next year. In 1205 Hōjō Tokimasa retired and was succeeded by his son, Yoshitoki, who received the title of *Shikken* and ruled in conjunction with his sister, Masago, Yoritomo's widow. Brinkley[2] says that "these were a great pair," who, by good government, "won a high place in the esteem and love of the people." In 1219 Sanetomo was assassinated by Yoriiye's son in revenge for his father's death, and ended the direct line from Yoritomo. From 1220 begins the line of so-called "Shadow Shōguns," who were mostly children of the Fujiwara family or the imperial house. "The situation of affairs in Japan at this time was deplorable." The Hōjō family "ruled both at Kyōto and Kamakura with resistless authority," which culminated in such a hitherto "unprecedented incident of Japanese history" as interference with the order of imperial succession. But, when once such a precedent had been established, it was not difficult to find a good excuse for repeating the performance.

---

[1] See Aston, *History of Japanese Literature.*

[2] *Japan, Its History, Arts and Literature*, II, 11.

Hōjō Yasutoki, who was *Shikken* from 1224 to 1242, was a man of great ability. "He was a true friend of the farmer in his seasons of famine and trial and a promoter of legal reforms and the arts." He gave up part of each month to hearing complaints. Anyone who had a complaint or petition need only strike a bell which hung in front of the Record Office, and he would receive prompt attention. Hōjō Yasutoki drew up a code of fifty-one articles, which "may be called a combination of a constitution, a criminal code, a civil code, and a code of civil procedure."

His grandson, Tokiyori, was also an able ruler, who "practiced economy in his administration and showed much consideration for the agricultural classes." In 1256 he retired to a monastery and delivered the regency to his son Tokimune. But the latter, being only six years old, was under the care of a tutor, Nagatoki, of the Hōjō family. "Thus it had come about that a tutor now controlled the Regent; who was supposed to control the Shōgun; who was supposed to be the vassal of the Emperor; who, in turn, was generally a child under the control of a corrupt and venal Court. Truly, government in Japan had sunk to its lowest point!"[1]

It was in the time of the regency of Tokimune (1268- 1281), and of the reign of the Emperor Go-Uda (Uda II, 1274-1287), in the year 1281, that an event occurred which, temporarily at least, quieted factional strife and united the Japanese nation in self-defense. This was an attempted invasion of Japan by the Mongol hordes of Kublai Khan.[2] A large fleet of Chinese junks, armed with catapults and other engines of destruction new to the Japanese, brought an army estimated at 100,000 men, and attacked Dazaifu, on the island of Kiūshiu. Then ensued a terrible contest, the outcome of which was for a while doubtful.

---

[1] Murray, *Japan*, p. 155.

[2] A previous invasion on a smaller scale in 1274 had been unsuccessful.

In fact, rumors circulated that the invaders had overrun Kiūshiu and were pushing on to Kyōto! "From the monasteries and temples all over the country went up unceasing prayer to the gods to ruin their enemies and save the land of Japan. The Emperor and ex-Emperor went in solemn state to the chief priest of Shintō, and, writing out their petitions to the gods, sent him as a messenger to the shrines at Ise."[1] These petitions seem to have been answered by the wind-god, who sent a typhoon, which, like the storm which saved England from the Spanish Armada, preserved Japan from the Tartar Armada. "Thus the only serious attempt at the invasion of Japan which has ever been made was completely frustrated" – by a "Divine Wind."

One interesting outcome of this Mongol invasion was that the Venetian traveler, Marco Polo, who happened to be living then at the Court of Kublai Khan, was able to learn something about Japan and publish it in his book. That was about the first information obtained by Europeans concerning Japan.

About the same time the Hōjō power was enhanced, and the dependence of the imperial house upon the Hōjō regents became more marked, when the latter made arrangement that two lines of the imperial family should reign alternately, so that neither line might become too powerful.

There now ensues a period of three or four decades without any event of importance, up to the time of the Regent Takatoki (1316-1326) and the Emperor Daigo II (Go-Daigo, 1318-1339). The latter was an able man, "who had acquired intimate knowledge of politics during many years of life as Prince Imperial," and "had conceived plans for restoring the reality of administrative power to the throne." The first result of this attempt was victory for the Hōjō, who, in 1330, banished the

---

[1] Griffis, *The Mikado's Empire*, p. 178. See also Murdoch, *History of Japan*, I, 524.

Emperor to the island of Oki,[1] and set up a successor, who is not, however, officially recognized as having reigned.

Now two famous characters appear on the scene of action: they are Nitta Yoshisada and Kusunoki Masashige, who, together, and with the aid of Ashikaga Takauji, succeeded in effecting the restoration of the exiled Emperor. Nitta, moreover, led an army against Kamakura, which, by taking advantage of ebb-tide, he was able to attack from three sides. After a severe and bloody contest the loyalist forces gained the victory, the Hōjō regent committed suicide, and the Hōjō Tyranny was at an end (1333).

Moreover, the city of Kamakura, "with its great triumphs of architecture, was almost entirely destroyed"; and little remained of "all the beauty and magnificence of Yoritomo's proud capital,... the first city in the Empire,... the home of all that was best in art and literature, in the refinement and luxury of life, as well as of trade and industry."[2] And, in 1915, there is not much left to show that Kamarura was once such a flourishing place.

While the political affairs of this period are saddening, there is something worthy of record in the progress of art. As it was an era of sanguinary warfare, it is natural that the manufacture of the sword, called "the soul of the *samurai,*" should have been well developed. It was in the reign of Go-Daigo that Masamune, the greatest of all swordsmiths, and his pupil, Muramasa, flourished. Dick says: "The Japanese blades are unsurpassed by the most famous swords of Damascus, India, and Persia; and the craft of the swordsmith was looked on as the most honourable of all handicrafts."[3] And Brinkley says: "If the Japanese had never produced anything but this sword (katana), they would still

---

[1] See Griffis, *The Mikado's Empire*, pp. 152, 153.

[2] Longford, *Story of Old Japan*, p. 145.

[3] *Arts and Crafts of Old Japan*, pp. 84, 87.

deserve to be credited with a remarkable faculty for detecting the subtle causes of practical effects, and translating them with delicate accuracy into obdurate material."[1]

This is also the period in which lived Katō, who spent six years (from 1223) in China studying the methods practiced there, and is called "the father of Japanese pottery."

The tea-plant had been first brought to Japan early in the ninth century, but had become practically unknown.

It was reintroduced near the end of the twelfth century, when it came immediately into general use.

This period of the glory of Kamakura is naturally the one in which was wrought the Dai Butsu, or Great Buddha, of that place.

This is also the period of Unkei, who, according to Dillon, "is probably the greatest sculptor that Japan has produced."

Strange as it may seem, this sanguinary era was one of large development of Buddhism. Four new sects, all of which have remained powerful to the present day, originated in the thirteenth century.

The Zenshiu, or Contemplative sect, "seeks salvation by meditation and a divine emptiness," so that, as Dr. Knox adds: "Its favorite hymn might well be 'Oh, to be nothing, nothing.' "[2] It arose as a reaction against the multiplication of idols, and "indicated a return to simpler forms of worship and conduct." Its doctrines may be summed up in the following injunction: "Look carefully within, and there you will find the Buddha." Its disciples have been variously called "Quietists," "Quakers," "Mystics"; and yet this creed also "immediately attracted the *samurai*"! This was largely due to the fact that, in Zen, each believer must work out his own salvation by austere discipline

---

[1] *Japan; Its History, Arts and Literature*, II, 136.

[2] *The Development of Religion in Japan*, p. 100.

and could thus develop the measure of self-control needed by a true knight.

The Jōdo, or Pure Land, sect was the first to teach the doctrine of salvation by faith in Amida. The Pure Land is a kind of Paradise, where Amida lives. And the only way to enter that heaven is "to cleave to Amida." This sect requires a simple rule of life in the frequent repetition of the phrase *Namu Amida Butsu* ("Glory to Amida the Buddha"). It is perhaps needless to add that being thus carried to heaven "on flowery beds of ease" made this sect very popular! It was "really a religion of despair rather than of hope" – a religion of self-abandonment.

But one of the disciples of the founder of the Jōdo sect established what he called "Jōdo Shinshiu," or "The True Sect of Jōdo." Later, however, the connection with Jōdo was lost, and the new sect has since been known merely as Shinshiu ("True Sect"), or Ikkōshiu ("Only Sect"). It also preaches justification by faith in Amida, and is in many respects "the Protestantism of Buddhism."[1] It is very liberal, as it abandons fasting, celibacy, isolation from society, penances, pilgrimages, charms, and amulets. It teaches that "morality is of equal importance with faith," i.e., that faith and works are co-ordinate. Knox, in his book, mentioned above, says: "It remains the largest and the most influential, the most zealous, and, unburdened by a cosmology or a philosophy, most able to adapt itself to modern conditions."

The latest sect is the one known as the Hokke, or the Nichiren, sect. The former name is derived from the name of its principal Sutra ("Holy Book"); the latter comes from the name of its founder. Its constant formula is the phrase, *Namu-myōhō-renge-kyō* ("Oh, the Sutra of the Lotus of the Wonderful Law"). It teaches "a form of pantheism, pure and simple: the Buddha is all,

---

[1] It is also sometimes called "Reformed Buddhism."

and all is Buddha." The whole life of its founder, Nichiren, is full of miracle and wonderful adventure, of which the most marvelous was his escape from death at the hands of the executioner sent by Hōjō Takayori.[1] Murdoch calls Nichiren "a strange compound of old Hebrew prophet, Dominican friar, and John Knox." He also says that Nichiren's preaching "undoubtedly did much to stimulate a spirit of nationality."[2] The disciples of Nichiren, following their master, are the most bigoted and intolerant of sectarians, the "high-church Buddhists," "the Jesuits of Japan." On account of their appeal to "what strikes the eye and the ear," they have been called "the Salvation Army of Buddhism." They foster the use of charms and amulets and believe in demoniacal possession.

---

[1] Griffis, *The Mikado's Empire*, p. 165.

[2] *History of Japan*, I, 483, 484, 501-3.

CHAPTER VII. ASHIKAGA ANARCHY

1333-1573 A.D.

The name of this period was not chosen for the sake of "apt alliteration's artful aid." It really depicts the state of affairs. With lack of authority, with insubordination, with the strife of rival claimants to the throne, and with frequent collisions between the feudal lords, it was truly a period of anarchy in every sense of that word. This period has also been appropriately called the "Dark Age" of Japan; and it includes the Namboku Chō Period (1332-1392) and the Muromachi Period (1392-1603). The former is so called because it was the period of the two rival Courts, the Southern *(Nan)* and the Northern *(Hoku)*; and the latter obtained its name from the fact that the Ashikaga Shōguns established their headquarters at Muromachi in Kyōto.

The first few years of this period are called the era of Temporary Imperialism (1333-1336), because for that very brief interval the Emperor Go-Daigo (Daigo II) was restored to power as the real ruler of the Empire. "But the Emperor Go-Daigo, however brave in adversity, was not wise in prosperity." To the popular heroes and true patriots, like Kusunoki and Nitta, he gave smaller rewards than to the schemer Ashikaga Takauji. This caused discontent among the soldiers, and Kusunoki and Nitta soon became embroiled in a contest with Ashikaga. The latter, by means of superior forces, overcame these generals, both of whom committed suicide. Kusunoki met his death at the battle of the Minato River, near Hiōgo, in 1336, and Nitta perished near Fukui in 1338. Both of these men are honored as real heroes; and Kusunoki, also known as Nankō, figures in Japanese history as the ideal patriot. He is "regarded to this day as the highest and noblest model that Japan has produced of the still higher quality of unselfish and devoted loyalty, the quality which, in the Japanese moral code, ranks far above any other, even that of filial piety."[1]

Ashikaga Takauji, "the central figure of the greatest political disturbance Japan ever knew," although he did not receive the title of Shōgun for several years, was now in absolute power. In 1336 the Emperor Daigo II was once more driven out of Kyōto and found refuge in the mountains of Yoshino, where the Southern Dynasty, with the imperial insignia and recognized as the legitimate line, "starved out a miserable existence" till 1392. Ashikaga, on the plea that Daigo II had forfeited the throne, set up a new emperor, known as Kōmyō, who, with the succeeding emperors of the Northern Dynasty, "enjoyed the luxury of a palace and of the capital," but are regarded as the illegitimate line. This period of two rival Courts *(Namboku Chō)* was one of "almost incessant fighting," which is denominated the "War of the Chrysanthemums." As Brinkley expresses it, "there is no blacker period of Japan's history."

Murdoch has most aptly characterized the period of the "War of the Chrysanthemums" as the "Great Age of Turncoats."[2] He shows that there were very few families that "remained constant" to either side in the contest.

But, as it was imperative to espouse one side or the other, it was not an uncommon custom for different branches of one family to espouse opposing causes and "carry on a friendly family warfare"! Then, in case of a decisive victory on one side or the other, the confiscated lands of the vanquished would pass "to friends and relatives"! Murdoch also points out two natural results of this internecine strife: first, "respect for central authority kept on waning;" and secondly, "every sect strong enough to do so endeavored to establish an *imperium in imperio*

---

[1] Longford, *Story of Old Japan*, pp. 154, 155.

[2] *History of Japan*, I, 564-6.

63

on its own behalf." All these things tended toward the development of the feudal system in Japan.

But there are bright sides of this "Dark Age"; for, when the country began to be impoverished by the civil strife, "the provincial nobles sought to replenish their exchequers by engaging in trade with China and Korea"; and the "custom of officially recognized trading ships came into vogue."

Moreover, many of the Ashikaga Shōguns were men of refinement and encouraged art. There was Yoshimitsu, who nominally served from 1368 to 1394 and lived in retirement in Kyōto till 1409. His palace was the three-storied building Kinkakuji (Golden Pavilion), a portion of which still evokes wonder on account of its elegance. Indeed, according to Brinkley, this was, for Kyōto, "its zenith of glory." Yoshimitsu also deserves great credit for "reconciling the two Courts and putting an end to the dual monarchy by prevailing upon the Southern Emperor, Go-Kameyama (Kameyama II), to come to Kyōto in 1392, to go into retirement, and acknowledge the Northern Emperor, Go-Komatsu (Komatsu II), as his legal successor with the insignia." This brought an interval of peace, during which the country had an opportunity to recover somewhat from its disturbed condition. In the middle of the fifteenth century (1443-1474) the Shōgun was Yoshimasa, who has been called "Japan's foremost dilettante," because he encouraged aestheticism in so many forms. He abdicated in order to be able the better to devote himself to a life of pleasure. He is the one who erected the Silver Pavilion (Ginkakuji), which is still one of the sights of Kyōto. Its garden was laid out by Sōami, "one of the greatest masters of landscape gardening" and a famous tea-professor. But all such luxuries are expensive, and, "when Yoshimasa wanted money, whether to build a pavilion, lay out a park, or purchase objects of virtu from China, he never scrupled about the means of getting it."[1]

In Yoshimasa's day, also, civil war broke out again over the double question of succession to the imperial throne and to the Shōgunate and raged fiercely for over ten years (1467-1477), at the end of which time "Kyōto lay almost in ruins." It was especially unfortunate that temples and palaces containing "magnificent works of art and valuable manuscripts" were destroyed.

By this time the control of the central administration was completely destroyed, and each local chief, though not nominally a "king," yet was "possessed of virtual regal powers."

While the Ashikaga Shōguns were living in luxury, the emperors were generally suffering with poverty. Indeed, in 1500, when the Emperor Tsuchi-mikado II died, his corpse lay unburied for forty days, simply because means were not at hand to perform the proper funeral rites! His son had to obtain money from Buddhist priests to defray the cost of his accession ceremonies. And the next emperor was compelled, not only to borrow money for a similar purpose, but even to support himself by selling his autograph, or by copying extracts from classic literature, or by writing poems or songs! And children "modelled mud toys" even "by the sides of the main approach to the imperial pavilion."

Moreover, the national dignity "had suffered badly from the fact that Yoshimitsu had not only accepted from the Chinese Emperor the title of King of Japan, but even paid him a tribute of one thousand ounces of gold." This was likewise the period when Japanese of Kifishiu became pirates, "swarmed along the coast of Asia from Tartary to Siam," and created tremendous consternation, especially in Korea and China. And, "about the middle of the Ashikaga Epoch, Matsumae Nobuhiro crossed to

---

[1] Brinkley, *Japan; Its History, Arts and Literature*, VI, 153.

the island of Ezo (Yezo), and he and his descendants brought the aborigines of that place into subjection."

In 1542 the Portuguese first came to Japan, to which they introduced tobacco, firearms, and Christianity in its Roman Catholic form. The pioneer Christian missionary was Francis Xavier, who landed at Kagoshima August 15, 1549, and thus opened what has been called "the Christian century" (1549-1638) in Japan. Xavier himself stayed in Japan only a little over two years, when he returned to China. He took with him two Japanese body-servants, one of whom died at Goa, but the other, "most likely the first Japanese who ever set foot in Europe," reached Lisbon and Rome, became a member of the "Society of Jesus," and died at Coimbra. Other Jesuit missionaries were sent to Japan, where they soon made many converts, especially in the island of Kiūshiu. It may not be possible to accept the claims of the Catholics concerning the number of converts, but it is absolutely certain that they were numerous and powerful. By 1567 it was asserted that in Nagasaki "there was hardly a person who was not a Christian." And, as one has put it, "it was in 1573 that Nagasaki became distinctively a Christian city."

In the latter half of the sixteenth century there came into prominence five great nobles (Takeda Shingen, Uyesugi Kenshin, Ōda Nobunaga, Hashiba Hideyoshi,[1] and Tokugawa Iyeyasu). In Brinkley's opinion, "this quintette saved Japan," for, "without them she must have become divided into a number of principalities, as her neighbor Korea had been, and like Korea she might have lost many of the qualities that make for national greatness."

The struggles between Takeda and Uyesugi are very interesting but only indirectly affected the affairs of the Empire at large. But the other three men became truly "national

---

[1] Afterward named Toyotomi Hideyoshi.

characters," a triumvirate of more than local power and influence. Of these, Nobunaga appeared first on the public stage. In 1568 Ashikaga Yoshiaki became Shōgun with Nobunaga's help and made the latter Vice Shōgun. With the added power and prestige of this position, Nobunaga subdued several other feudal lords; destroyed the famous monastery on Hieizan, near Kyōto, because the monks thereof sided with his enemies;[1] and in 1573 defeated the Shōgun himself, with whom ended the Ashikaga Dynasty.

Concerning this period Aston[2] says that it was "singularly barren of important literature." Chikafusa, one of the statesmen who faithfully served the Emperor Daigo II, wrote a *History of the True Succession of the Divine Monarchs*, who were, of course, those of the Southern Dynasty. *Taiheiki*, or "Great Peace Record," was "the strange name for the history of one of the most disturbed periods that Japan has ever passed through"; it also upholds the Southern Dynasty. But the classic of the period is *Tsurezure-gusa*, which means literally "Leisure-Hour-Grasses." "It is a collection of short sketches, anecdotes, and essays on all imaginable subjects, something in the manner of Selden's *Table Talks.*"[3]

This was also a period of great popularity of the Nō or lyrical drama. Yoshimasa gave it a new impetus "by officially declaring it a ceremonious accomplishment of military men." The great similarity between Nō and the ancient Greek drama cannot be left unnoticed. "The chorus, the masked actors, the religious tone pervading the piece, the stage in the open air – all these features

---

[1] They "hatched plots to light or fan the flames of feudal war, so as to make the quarrels of the clans and chiefs redound to their aggrandizement." And they "trusted profoundly to their professedly sacred character to shield them from all danger, but in vain; for Nobunaga had no respect for them" (Griffis).

[2] *History of Japanese Literature.*

[3] See Sansom translation in Vol. XXXIX of the *Transactions of the Asiatic Society of Japan.*

were common to the two dramas."[1]

The barrenness of this period in literature is counterbalanced by its fecundity in art. The scope of the aesthetic development may be seen in the fact that it was a glorious era for architecture, landscape gardening, decorative painting, the tea-cult, the flower cult, the incense cult, and the Nō, most of which, as we have seen, Yoshimasa lavishly patronized. It is only in Japan that landscape gardening can be said to be "reduced almost to an exact science." And Japan seems also to be the only land where incense burning and tea drinking are likewise systematized. The tea ceremony (Cha-no-yu) is of special interest; "four cardinal virtues constituted the basis of Shukō's system: they were urbanity, courtesy, purity, and imperturbability."[2]

This was naturally a great period for swordsmiths and workers in metal for armor, etc. In this line the Miōchin family demands special mention.

The Old Yamato School of decorative painters was merged into the Tosa Academy, "whose members carried the art of pictorial decoration to an extraordinary degree of elaboration and splendor."[3] Chō Densu, "the Fra Angelico of Japan," lived from 1351 to 1427, and "devoted himself to sacerdotal art." Sesshiu, during a trip to China, only to learn nothing from the masters there, said: "Nature shall be my teacher; I shall go to the woods, the mountains, and the streams and learn from them."[4] He became "one of the greatest of all Japanese painters"; and, with Masanobu and Matanobu, represents the Kano School.

It is worth while to note, in passing, that, "by an interesting coincidence, Japanese painting attained its acme synchronously with Italian art, that is to say, during the fifteenth century," when

---

[1] Brinkley, *Japan; Its History, Arts and Literature*, III, 30, 31.

[2] Brinkley, *Japan; Its History, Arts and Literature*, II, 252, 253.

[3] *Ibid.*, II, 66.

[4] Dick, *Arts and Crafts of Old Japan*.

Sesshiu flourished (1421-1507).

It really seems paradoxical that not only aestheticism in so many forms, but also mysticism, as represented in the contemplative Zen sect, which "attracted the *samurai,*" should have flourished in the midst of the Ashikaga Anarchy.

CHAPTER VIII. CIVIL STRIFE

1573-1603 A.D.

In characterizing this period as one of civil strife,[1] there is no intention to suggest that other periods were free from that element. Nor does it necessarily mean that this was pre-eminently an era of civil strife: it only means that, immediately after the Ashikaga Anarchy, there was a very important period of about three decades which was marked by a severe conflict to decide who should finally bring tranquillity out of warfare, order out of anarchy. In accomplishing this there were several minor and three principal actors, all of whom were mentioned in the preceding chapter. The three principal agents in unifying Japan were Ōda Nobunaga, Toyotomi Hideyoshi, and Tokugawa Iyeyasu, the latter two of whom were at first generals under Nobunaga.

When Ōda Nobunaga, at the age of sixteen, had succeeded to his father's small estates in Owari, his prospects were not at all brilliant, and "he himself gave such scant signs of promise that he was usually referred to by the nickname of ' Bakadono' or 'Lord Fool.' " But gradually, with the assistance of Hideyoshi and Iyeyasu, he was enabled to extend his dominions and power, until he finally became master of Kyōto and Vice-Shōgun, "with the Shōgun merely his puppet." In 1573, as we have seen, Nobunaga deposed the Shōgun, "although he did not actually strip him of his title." He could not himself take that title, because he did not belong to the Minamoto family,[2] but he assumed the duties of the office, i.e., "he issued orders and made

---

[1] The fullest account of the events of this period is found in the *History of Japan*, by Murdoch and Yamagata.

[2] He was a Taira.

war and formed alliances in the name of the Emperor."

Nevertheless, Nobunaga had to fight to maintain himself in his lofty position. It is true that the death of the great Takeda Shingen in 1573 "was a stroke of the most consummate good luck for Nobunaga." And, as Brinkley has well expressed it, Takeda's exploits, while very interesting, "need not be considered here further than to say that they contributed materially to regenerate the era and to restore the nation's ideal of soldierly qualities."[1] Uyesugi Kenshin continued the contest against Nobunaga a few years longer, until his death in 1578; and Takeda Katsuyori, son of the old hero, was not finally overcome till 1582.

The hardest struggle, however, which Nobunaga had was that with the monks of the Shin sect in Ōsaka. How he destroyed the monastery on Hieizan has already been related in the preceding chapter. At different intervals, for several years, Nobunaga attacked Osaka, but in vain; for the head-priest (Kenniō) had so fortified the monastery there that it was one of the strongest fortresses in that section of the country. In 1580, however, after a long siege, attended by dreadful slaughter, the fortress surrendered.

In 1579 "Nobunaga had been enabled to deal another Buddhist sect a staggering blow." He was called upon to act as judge in a contest between priests of the Jōdo and the Nichiren sects. "The discussion, famous as the *Azuchi Ron,* took place in Nobunaga's new castle of Azuchi," which he had begun to build in 1576. Nobunaga decided against the Nichiren sect, upon which he inflicted terrible punishment.

While Nobunaga was apparently an enemy of Buddhists, he seemed to be a friend of the Christians; but probably it was not

---

[1] Brinkley, *Japan; Its History, Arts and Literature,* II, 34. Murdoch thinks that Takeda was "certainly a better man then Nobunaga".

because he loved Christianity more, but because he loved Buddhism less. At any rate, he befriended the Catholic priests and aided them in their propaganda by allowing them many privileges, especially in the way of building churches here and there. The natural result was that the number of converts rapidly increased in Sakai, Ōsaka, Kyōto, Takatsuki, and other places in Central Japan. It is not strange, therefore, that the Jesuits and their converts "began to regard Nobunaga as the chosen but unconscious instrument of God." "Some said that Nobunaga was a Christian; others that he was minded to become one; others that the Prince (his son Nobutada) had been baptized."[1]

It was in the flourishing days of Christianity, during Nobunaga's supremacy, that the celebrated embassy to the Pope started out from Nagasaki, but it did not reach Europe till 1584. It was received by Pope Gregory XIII only a few days before his death and assisted at the coronation of his successor. It did not return to Japan till 1590.

Not long after that embassy had left Japan, Nobunaga met his end. He had started out from Azuchi to assist Hideyoshi in the capture of the castle of Takamatsu in Sanuki on the island of Shikoku. He himself, with a small escort, went by way of Kyōto and temporarily stopped there in the temple of Honnōji. His general, Akechi, with the troops, had been sent a shorter way; but, saying to the troops, "My enemy is in the Honnōji," and promising them plunder, Akechi suddenly changed his line of march and attacked Nobunaga in the temple. The latter was able to defend himself only a short time, when, seeing that escape was hopeless, he committed *harakiri*. It is presumed that Akechi's action was in revenge for a "humiliating joke,"[2] by which

---

[1] See chap. vii of Murdoch and Yamagata *History of Japan*.

[2] Nobunaga is reported to have taken Akechi's head under his arm, and, using it like a drum, to have played a tune on it with his fan.

Nobunaga had offended him.

When Hideyoshi heard of Nobunaga's death, having secured the surrender of Takamatsu Castle, he hurried back to Kyōto, near which he fought a battle with Akechi. The latter was completely defeated and committed harakiri. His short-lived glory has been perpetuated in a proverb, "Akechi's three days."[1]

Hideyoshi was now the most prominent personage in Japan, and proceeded to strengthen himself in every way. For instance, in 1583 he began building the great Ōsaka Castle. "Workmen were drawn from all parts of Japan," and spent several years in the task. He also constructed at Fushimi, near Kyōto, a "Palace of Pleasure," called Momoyama,[2] which was demolished by an earthquake in 1596, but has given a name to this period in the history of Japanese art.

Hideyoshi was ambitious to become Shōgun; but, as he was a "base-born, monkey-faced adventurer," who did not belong to the noble family of Minamoto, he was ineligible.

In 1586, however, he received the title of Regent *(Kwampaku)*, which had hitherto been held exclusively by the aristocratic Fujiwara, and in 1591 that of Great Prince *(Taikō)*, by which he is best known in Japanese history.

The first great contest into which Hideyoshi was drawn was one with the Satsuma clan, which was even then famous for "bravery and dash." In 1587 Hideyoshi led such a large army into Kiūshiu that his enemies were completely outnumbered and compelled to retreat to Kagoshima. In all probability he could easily have captured the fortress and practically exterminated the Satsuma clan. But "it was at this juncture that Hideyoshi made one of these surprising and clever movements which stamp him

---

[1] It was really twelve days.

[2] This is the location of the mausoleum of the late Emperor Mutsuhito, now known as Meiji Tennō (1867-1912).

as a man of consummate genius." He was no longer a mere warrior; he became a real statesman. By imposing comparatively light terms, he obtained the submission of this mighty clan, whose allegiance was thus secured.[1]

In 1585, Pope Gregory XIII had issued a bull that "no religious teachers except Jesuits should be allowed in Japan." But, as "Japan was not Spain," this spirit of the Inquisition could not flourish or prevail. This bull only created jealousy in the hearts of the Dominicans and the Franciscans against the Jesuits and of the Spanish against the Portuguese. Wily Franciscans succeeded in getting into Japan "as ambassadors and not as religious teachers." These national and sectarian jealousies caused dissension in Christian circles in Japan. Moreover, an indiscreet remark by a European sea-captain that his master accomplished foreign conquests by first sending priests to win the people and then getting possession of the country through the native Christians, had aroused Hideyoshi's suspicions against foreigners in general and Christians in particular. Therefore, in 1587 he suddenly issued this edict:

> *Having learned from our faithful councillors, that*
> *foreign religieux have come into our estates, where*
> *they preach a law contrary to that of Japan, and that*
> *they have even had the audacity to destroy temples*
> *dedicated to our Kami[2] and Hotoke:[3] although this*
> *outrage merits the most extreme punishment,*
> *wishing nevertheless to show them mercy, we order*
> *them under pain of death to quit Japan within*
> *twenty days. During that space no harm or hurt will*

---

[1] See paper on "Hideyoshl and the Satsuma Clan in the Sixteenth Century", by Gubbins, in *Transactions of the Asiatic Society of Japan*, VIII, 92 f.

[2] Shintō gods.

[3] Buddhist gods.

be done them. But at the expiration of that time, we
order that, if any of them be found in our states, they
shall be seized and punished as the greatest
criminals. As for the Portuguese merchants, we
permit them to enter our ports, there to continue
their accustomed trade, and to remain in our states
provided our affairs need this. But we forbid them to
bring any foreign religieux into the country, under
the penalty of the confiscation of their ships and
goods.[1]

But it happened that the missionaries, driven out of central Japan, found refuge in Kiūshiu among the so called Christian clans, where that edict was not enforced.

Moreover, Hideyoshi's attention was soon directed elsewhere to a more important matter. In 1590 he led an army against Hōjō Ujimasu, who was the most powerful lord in the Kwantō section, with his headquarters at Odawara. That place was captured after a siege; and not only that section, but also Northern Japan, submitted to Hideyoshi, who "was now undisputed master of the Empire from Tanegashima in the south on to snowy Yezo in the north; the work of mere territorial centralization was complete." It was during this successful campaign that Hideyoshi suggested to Iyeyasu, to whom he intended to turn over several of those provinces, that Odawara was not the best place for his headquarters, but that a place called Yedo was better. He said: "It is girdled by rivers and the sea, and it is a fine position; and that is the place where I would that thou shouldst live." Twenty-five years later, Iyeyasu made Yedo his capital.

Hideyoshi's ambition was not limited to the islands of Japan, but extended to a foreign country. A Japanese adventurer, named Harada, having gone to the Philippines to trade,

---

[1] Murdoch and Yamagata, *History of Japan.*

suggested to Hideyoshi to require the Spanish governor of those islands to recognize him as suzerain. It is quite likely that the plan also contemplated the conquest of the Philippines; but it failed entirely.[1]

Hideyoshi is reported to have laid before Nobunaga a plan by which he would conquer Korea and China "as easily as a man rolls up a piece of matting and carries it under his arm." In 1592 he began the famous invasion of Korea with an immense army under the command of two generals, Konishi (a Christian) and Katō (a Buddhist). The two divisions marched together as far as the capital, but after taking possession thereof separated on account of dissensions. It is unnecessary to follow the details of the movements of the Japanese armies, which, meeting with both successes and reverses, remained in Korea till 1598, when they were recalled by Iyeyasu soon after Hideyoshi's death. One attempt to make peace had failed in 1596, because in the terms of the treaty it was stated that Hideyoshi was "invested" by the Chinese Emperor as "King of Japan" – a humiliation too great for a man like Hideyoshi to endure. In one of the last battles fought in Korea the ears and noses of several thousand Chinese and Korean soldiers were pickled in tubs and sent to Kyōto, where they were deposited in a mound, called *mimizuka* ("ear-mound"), which, with the monument over it, may still be seen. This is truly "a chapter in the history of Japan, on which her best friends can look back with neither pride nor satisfaction."[2]

One great benefit, however, indirectly accrued to Japan from this unjustifiable attack upon Korea. When Prince Shimazu, lord of the Satsuma clan, returned in 1598 from Korea, he brought with him seventeen skilled Korean potters, to whom the old

---

[1] See Clement's Hildreth, *Japan as It Was and Is*, I, chap. xiii.

[2] Murray, *Japan*, p. 221. See also Aston paper in *Transactions of the Asiatic Society of Japan*, Vol. VI.

Satsuma faience "owes its exquisite beauty and world-wide reputation" as "the most beautiful ware produced in Japan."

Hideyoshi's edict against Christian missionaries had, as we have seen, become practically a dead letter; but in 1597, for various reasons, his wrath was again directed toward the foreign priests. Twenty-six of them were crucified at Nagasaki in February of that year; and just thirty years later, these, the first Christian martyrs in Japan, were canonized by Pope Urban VIII.

It was in September, 1598, that Hideyoshi, the "Napoleon of Japan," "the greatest soldier, if not the greatest man, whom Japan has produced," passed away. Another foreign writer (Murdoch) calls him "the greatest man Japan has ever seen, and the greatest statesman of his century, whether in Japan or in Europe." The latter is impressed with

> the strength of his [Hideyoshi's] grasp upon the
> actualities of the situation, his unerring sense of
> political perspective, his prescience of the future and
> the problems it would present, and the grand unity,
> continuity, and comprehensiveness of his statecraft...
> The age of Taikō was one of great activity ... and
> deserves a history by itself. In many seas and countries
> of the East, Japanese voyaged or made settlements,...
> and carried far the fame of the great Taikō.[1]

Hideyoshi naturally desired to continue the power in his own family; but, as his son Hideyori was only five years old, it was necessary to appoint a council of five regents, of whom Iyeyasu was president. The other members of that body soon grew jealous of Iyeyasu's growing influence and power. "Events now rushed rapidly to a culmination." Iyeyasu met the combined

---

[1] Murdoch and Yamagata, *History of Japan*, pp. 301, 302. See also Brinkley, *Japan; Its History, Arts and Literature*, II, 35, 36, and Longford, *Story of Old Japan*, pp. 182, 184, 199.

forces of his opponents at Sekigahara in 1600 and completely vanquished them.[1] It was after this battle that he uttered that famous saying, which has become a proverb: "After victory, knot the cords of your helmet." And, suiting the action to the word, he followed up his victory by such speedy movements that his enemies submitted to him. In 1603 he received the title of Shōgun and proceeded to establish the Tokugawa Dynasty in that position.

Although Iyeyasu still has the most important part of his career ahead of him, this is a very convenient point at which to make a few comparisons between the famous triumvirs. It may be said that Nobunaga was a warrior, but not a statesman; that Hideyoshi was a warrior and a statesman; that Iyeyasu was a statesman and a warrior. The Japanese say that Nobunaga pounded the rice-cake *(mochi)*, that Hideyoshi cooked it, and that Iyeyasu sat on a cushion and ate it! There are also three verses to illustrate the characters of the three men:

Nobunaga is represented as saying,

> *Nakaneba korosu,*
> *Hototogisu.*

Hideyoshi follows with

> *Nakashite miyō,*
> *Hototogisu.*

This draws from Iyeyasu the words,

> *Naku made matō*
> *Hototogisu.*

---

[1] Longford (p. 210) calls this battle "the third of the great decisive battles of Japan." The first was Dan-no-ura, which "confirmed the absolute power of Yoritomo"; the second, Minato River, "that of Takauji"; the third "made Iyeyasu master of all Japan."

Nobunaga said, "I'll kill the cuckoo, if he doesn't sing"; Hideyoshi, "I'll try and make the cuckoo sing"; and Iyeyasu said, "I'll wait till the cuckoo sings."

These couplets are said to represent well the characters and methods of the three men. "Nobunaga was headstrong and cruel. Hideyoshi believed that everything could be made to bend to his iron will... Iyeyasu was a past master in diplomacy. His motto was, 'All things come to him who can wait.' "[1]

In any event, each man played his part well and contributed toward the final pacification and unification which followed after this period of civil strife.

---

[1] Dening, *New Life of Toyotomi Hideyoshi*, pp. 222, 223.

CHAPTER IX. TOKUGAWA FEUDALISM, I

Organization (1603-1638)

We enter now upon a very important period in the history of Japan. It may also be called the Yedo Period, because its influences centered in the city of Yedo which Iyeyasu later selected as his capital. It is the period of the most perfect organization of Japanese feudalism. When Iyeyasu became Shōgun in 1603, he set himself to organize the central and the provincial governments in such a way as to maintain the power in his own family, and he succeeded in founding a dynasty which kept the administration of affairs for 265 years. As has already been pointed out in chap. v, the Tokugawa, unlike the Fujiwara, but like the Taira and the Minamoto, based their power "on the possession of armed strength which the throne had no competence to control"; transferred the center of political gravity "to a point altogether outside the Court, the headquarters of a military feudalism"; and thus "governed in spite of the Emperor." It is not within the limits of this book to go into the details of "the Tokugawa administrative machine," as it has been aptly labeled by Murdoch, who briefly describes it as "a most intricate and complicated system of governmental machinery, with checks and counter-checks and 'regulators' innumerable."[1]

There were three points of great importance: " first, to elaborate some system for the effective control of the feudal nobles; secondly, to establish a good understanding with the imperial Court in Kyōto; and thirdly, to organize the

---

[1] The most complete accounts may be found in Murdoch and Yamagata, *History of Japan*, chap. xviii, and Walter Dickson, *Japan*. See also a paper by Gubbins in *Transactions of the Asiatic Society of Japan*, Vol. XV.

administrative machinery in a skilful and permanent manner."[1]

The second point was accomplished

> *by giving, on the one hand, a full measure of*
> *recognition to the divinity of the throne's occupant,*
> *and by enforcing, on the other, the theological*
> *sequence of that doctrine... The imperial Court was*
> *organized in Kyōto with all pomp and circumstance;*
> *... but, as for the sovereign's actual power, it did not*
> *extend beyond... functions of no importance*
> *whatever... The control of [public] affairs rested*
> *absolutely in the hands of the Shōgun.*[2]

The first and third points were practically accomplished together. In the first place, all the feudal lords were divided into two classes: *fudai*, or vassals of the Tokugawa family, and *tozama*, or outside lords. Several of the former were relatives of the Tokugawa family, and most of them were especially honored with the name Matsudaira. Three of these formed the *Go-sanke*, or "Three Honorable Families," of Owari, Kii, and Mito, from which a Shōgun might be selected in case the main line failed. Among the *tozama*, the five most prominent princes were Kaga, Sendai, Aizu, Chōshu, and Satsuma, who enjoyed special privileges.

Iyeyasu also established a lower grade of nobility known as *hatamoto*, who had small holdings with varying incomes and held important official positions in the Shōgun's government. Below these was a still inferior class called *gokenin*; and again below these were the *samurai*, or the common soldiers. But even the *samurai* were the highest of the four classes of society. It was positively enjoined that the other three classes of "farmers, artisans, and merchants may not behave in a rude manner

---

[1] *Official History of the Empire of Japan.*

[2] *Ibid.*

toward *samurai.* "[1]

Moreover, Iyeyasu rearranged the feudal fiefs in such a way that the Emperor in Kyōto was practically encircled and imprisoned by Tokugawa vassals, while his own new city of Yedo, which was made his capital in 1615, was girded by friendly fiefs. Iyeyasu was an early adept at gerrymandering!

And later Iyemitsu compelled all the lords to reside in Yedo half of each year and kept their wives and children there as hostages; so that Tokugawa was absolutely supreme.

But there are other events to claim attention during this interesting period. On April 11, 1600, Will Adams, after an unfortunate voyage in a Dutch vessel called "De Liefde," landed on the coast of Bungo, in Kiūshiu, and thus was probably the first British subject to set foot in Japan. After a short imprisonment, during which the Portuguese tried by slander to compass his death, he was set at liberty and kept about the Shōgun's court, where he made himself useful in many ways, especially in shipbuilding. In 1605 Iyeyasu gave the captain of the "Liefde" a kind of "license for the Dutch nation to trade with Japan"; and eventually a Dutch vessel, "Red Lion," was dispatched to Japan, and arrived, on July 6, 1609, at Hirado. There a factory was established and carried on a more or less profitable business for about thirty years, when it was moved to Nagasaki.

It was also in 1609 that Don Rodrigo de Vivero, the retiring governor of the Philippines, when attempting to return to New Spain, was driven by a storm to Japan, and his vessel was completely wrecked off the coast of Bōshiu. He was kindly received by Iyeyasu, with whom he succeeded in concluding a kind of treaty of alliance, trade, and commerce with the king of Spain. In 1610 Japan sent her first ship to Mexico (New Spain);

---

[1] See the so-called "Legacy of Iyeyasu."

and Spanish trade with Japan was carried on for fourteen years (1610-1624).

It was only a few years later that, in accordance with instructions from the English East India Company, Captain John Saris, in the "Clove," arrived at Hirado (June 11, 1613), to open trade between England and Japan. Saris, too, received a cordial welcome from Iyeyasu and succeeded in negotiating a charter[1] granting privileges of trade. This led to the establishment of the English factory at Hirado; but, "after a troubled and troublous existence of ten years, it was finally dissolved."

This era was, indeed, a period of great commercial activity, when "wealthy traders of Kifishiu traveled abroad to a great extent for business purposes" and "great numbers of merchants came to Japan from Annam, Siam, Luzon, and other places of the south, as well as from the southern districts of China and from India."[2] During the last decade of the preceding century, as has been mentioned in the preceding chapter, a Japanese adventurer named Harada had gone to the Philippines to trade and had succeeded in filling Hideyoshi's ambitious mind with the wild plan of requiring the Spanish governor to acknowledge him (Hideyoshi) as sovereign. An imperious letter of that kind was actually written but never delivered. One Yamada, in the early part of the seventeenth century, got as far as Siam, where he organized the Japanese settlers, helped the king in quelling rebellions and in defeating a Spanish army which invaded Siam, and thus "rose to be Prime Minister of the Kingdom." But by 1633 "no Japanese vessel might go on a foreign voyage, except the nine vessels... that had special permits bearing the vermilion seal of the Shōgun." And in 1636 a set of regulations was issued

---

[1] See Clement's Hildreth, *Japan as It Was and Is*," I, 219, 220.

[2] *Official History of the Empire of Japan.*

limiting Japanese ships to 500 *koku* burden.[1] "And thus was the mercantile marine of Japan regulated off the face of the deep."

During the first years of the Tokugawa Feudalism the government showed no hostility to Christianity, so that until 1612 "no Japanese Christian had suffered merely on account of being a Christian." But from that year several suffered on account of being mixed up in political intrigues. In January, 1614, Iyeyasu delivered his first and last blow at Christianity by an edict that "the members of all religious orders, whether European or Japanese, should be sent out of the country; that the churches which had been erected in various localities should be pulled down; and that the native adherents of the faith should be compelled to renounce it."[2]

The year before that edict was issued Date, the powerful chief of the Sendai clan, had sent a prominent Japanese Christian, named Hasekura, together with Sotelo, a Franciscan friar, on an embassy to the Pope. They had audience of Pope Paul V on November 30, 1615; but Hasekura did not return to Japan till 1620, and afterward renounced his faith.

Meantime, Hideyoshi's son, Hideyori, living in Osaka in great style, and possessing considerable influence, threatened the life of the Tokugawa Dynasty. As early as 1605 Iyeyasu had nominally retired from the position of Shōgun and had 'been succeeded by his own son, Hidetada; but the veteran still kept his hand on affairs by acting as regent. And, as the growing influence of the Taikō's son seriously threatened his own family, and as Ōsaka seemed to be a center of rally for all disaffected persons, Iyeyasu picked a quarrel by pretending to be offended by the inscriptions[3] on the new bell of a temple in Kyōto. No

---

[1] One *koku* is almost five bushels.

[2] Murray, *Japan*, p. 246.

[3] It was claimed that they contained disrespectful allusions to Iyeyasu himself.

explanations on the part of Hideyori's friends were accepted, and in 1614 Iyeyasu set out from Suruga (now Shizuoka), his home in retirement, with a large army against Osaka. The castle there was so bravely defended that it seemed practically impregnable. But Hideyori's leaders foolishly decided to stake all on a great battle outside and were completely overthrown. Hideyori then committed suicide. "So fell Ōsaka Castle; and so was the House of Toyotomi destroyed."

Iyeyasu did not long survive this final victory, but died the following year (1616). And in 1617 his body was interred in the tomb prepared at Nikkō, which has since become so famous both for its natural and for its artificial beauties. And among the decorators of that tomb was Hidari Jingoro, "the left-handed carpenter who became the greatest wood-carver of the day," and who is the only person worthy of mention in connection with the art of the sub-period under consideration. He has been called "the Japanese Phidias" and is most famous for his sleeping cat, in which he seems to have succeeded in showing in wood " the fine and very delicate distinction between death and sleeping life."

While Iyeyasu was a general of great ability, he was more of a constructive statesman: his talent lay in "consolidating the power which had been acquired by his predecessor." Murdoch says: "What strikes one most in connection with Iyeyasu is his consummate judgment. If genius can be accurately defined as an infinite capacity for taking pains, then Tokugawa Iyeyasu was certainly possessed of a large measure of genius." Moreover, quite unlike Nobunaga or Hideyoshi, he was inclined to literature and became "the noted patron of learned men." He gathered scholars around him; "caused the Confucian classics to be printed"[1]; and generally favored education, of which these classics were the essential part. They consisted of the Four Books

---

[1] Probably for the first time in Japan.

(*The Great Learning*, *The Doctrine of the Mean*, *The Confucian Analects*, and *The Sayings of Mencius*) and the Five Canons (The Book of Changes, The Book of Poetry, The Book of History, The Canon of Rites, and Spring and Autumn).

Iyeyasu's son and successor, Hidetada, insisted on the enforcement of the anti-Christian edict of 1614, at the evasion of which some of the lords had connived; and he sent several foreign priests and many Japanese Christians to death. Gubbins, in his paper on *The Introduction of Christianity into China and Japan*,"[1] writes as follows:

> We read of Christians being executed in a barbarous
> manner in sight of each other, of their being hurled
> from the tops of precipices, of their being buried alive,
> of their being torn asunder by oxen, of their being
> tied up in rice-bags, which were heaped up together,
> and of the pile thus formed being set on fire. Others
> were tortured before death by the insertion of sharp
> spikes under the nails of their hands and feet, while
> some poor wretches, by a refinement of horrid
> cruelty, were shut up in cages and there left to starve
> with food before their eyes.

In 1622 occurred what is known as the "Great Martyrdom" at Nagasaki. "This name it well deserves on account of the number, dignity, and illustrious virtue of the victims, and the atrocious torments many of them endured."[2] "Thirty Christians were beheaded, and twenty-five others, among them nine foreign priests, literally roasted to death, for their tortures lasted between two and three hours."

The following year (1623) Hidetada nominally retired in favor of his son, Iyemitsu, but "continued to wield the real

---

[1] *Transactions of the Asiatic Society of Japan*, Vol. VI.

[2] See Wilberforce, *Dominican Missions and Martyrs in Japan*.

authority down to his death in 1632." There was, moreover, no break in the continuity of the persecution of the Christians. In 1633 the new "torment of the fosse," or pit, was devised, which was truly of "the most devilish ingenuity." "A hole was dug in the ground, over which a gallows was erected. From this gallows the sufferer, swathed in bandages, was suspended by his feet, being lowered for half his length, head downward, into the hole, which was then closed by two boards which fitted together around the victim so as to exclude the light and air."[1] About this time also was instituted a method of inquisition of "detestable solemnity " to distinguish Christians from non-believers. Everyone (man, woman, or child) was required to trample on an image of the Savior or of the Virgin Mary. If any refused, they were at once turned over to the proper officials for torture.

This "reign of terror," combined with "economic troubles," finally resulted in what is known as the great Christian revolt of Shimabara (1637-1638). A large number of Christians (men, women, and children) bravely withstood the attacks of the Shōgun's forces for two and one-half months, but finally, on April 12, 1638, were overwhelmed, and "massacred incontinently." This "practically extirpated Christianity in Japan for more than two centuries."[2]

And, to the shame of the Dutch in Hirado, it must be recorded that, "to save at any price the commerce with Japan," the head of the Dutch factory there took one of his ships and bombarded the castle in which the Christians made their final stand.

Meantime, in 1636, regulations had been promulgated by Iyemitsu to the effect that "all vessels of sea-going capacity should be destroyed, and that no craft should thenceforth be

---

[1] See Clement's Hildreth, *Japan as It Was and Is*, pp. 241-48.

[2] See Murdoch and Yamagata, *History of Japan*, chap. xxii.

built of sufficient size to venture beyond home waters."

Two years later (1638), because the Portuguese were suspected of having fomented the Shimabara revolt, an edict was issued that forbade any of the Portuguese to set foot on Japanese soil or to enter any Japanese harbor on any pretext whatsoever. "Henceforth... all Portuguese ships coming to Japan were to be burned, together with their cargoes, and everyone on board of them to be executed."[1] And such punishment was inflicted in 1640 upon some envoys from Macao. A few of the suite were spared to carry back the news to Macao; and they were shown a tablet with the following inscription:

> So long as the sun warms the earth, let no Christian
> be so bold as to come to Japan, and let all know that
> if King Philip himself, or even the very God of the
> Christians, or the great Shaka [Buddha] contravene
> this prohibition, they shall pay for it with their
> heads![2]

In spite of attempts made by the Portuguese in 1639, 1640, and 1649 to renew trade with Japan, the old relations were never resumed. And when a Japanese writer tried to take stock of the results of the century of foreign intercourse, he counts up only "the adoption of gunpowder and firearms as weapons, the use of tobacco and the habit of smoking, the making of sponge-cake (and bread?), the naturalization into the language of a few foreign words, and the introduction of new and strange forms of disease."[3]

Furthermore, the Dutch were compelled in 1641 to remove from Hirado to the small isle of Deshima, off Nagasaki, where they were practically imprisoned, but allowed to trade with one

---

[1] See Clement's Hildreth, *Japan as It Was and Is*, I, 249.

[2] Version given by Murdoch and Yamagata.

[3] Professor Shiga *History of Nations*, quoted by Murray in his *Japan*, p. 267.

ship per year. It is a euphemism (or a joke) to call Deshima even a "small isle"; it was in fact only six hundred feet long and two hundred and forty feet wide. In this narrow spot, which was inclosed with high boards, covered with a projecting roof so that only high hills were visible, the Dutch were literally cooped up and held like prisoners. But they were willing to undergo all kinds of humiliation for the sake of the trade monopoly.[1]

And, as Japanese were also prohibited from going abroad, Japan entered upon a period of seclusion, with two phases of exclusion and inclusion. Thus, although Japan was perhaps preserved from becoming a Catholic nation, Iyemitsu "arrested Japan's international development which then seemed full of promise," and doomed his country to a sleep of over two centuries.

---

[1] See Longford, *Story of Old Japan*, pp. 286-90.

CHAPTER X. TOKUGAWA FEUDALISM, II

Sleep of Japan (1638-1853)

This Period has received various appellations and characterizations. Though it was not completely free from insurrections and bloodshed, it has appropriately been called an era of "Great Peace." It was the period, as Okakura expresses it,[1] of the "hibernation of Japan within her chrysalis," when "we [Japanese] were as one buried alive," and when "every element of individuality was crushed under the weight of unbending formalism." And he adds: "Our life grew to be like those miniature and dwarf trees that were typical products of the Tokugawa Age." In like manner, the late Count Terashima, when Foreign Minister, once, "pointing to a grove of fir trees which had been trimmed and trained by generations of gardeners into quaint and not unpleasing but stunted shapes," said to Aston[2]: "There is an emblem of the Japanese nation under the Bakufu (Shōgunate). That is what Chinese learning did for us." This period, to quote Okakura again, "affords the peculiar spectacle of a society perfectly isolated and self-complete, which, acting and reacting upon itself, produced worlds within worlds, each with its separate life and ideals, and its own distinct expressions in art and literature." But this time of "self- concentration" was not unnaturally a Renaissance in literature and art, an era of the "Revival of Learning," or at least "the Golden Era of Chinese literature in Japan." And from some points of view this may truly be called the time when Japan reached "the acme of her ancient greatness," especially in the arts of peace.

---

[1] *The Awakening of Japan*, chap. ii.
[2] *History of Japanese Literature.*

One writer[1] has said that "the history of the Tokugawa Period is, politically speaking, a singularly uneventful one"; and he adds that, "apart from fires and earthquakes, there are few striking events for the annalist to record." Nevertheless this era is one worthy of special study. And at the very outset one interesting point must be noted, that all the history centers around the Shōguns, while the emperors or empresses are comparatively figureheads.

It was, as we have seen, under the administration of Iyemitsu, the Third Shōgun, that both the internal and the external policies of Japan were crystallized. During the period of the Fourth Shōgun (Iyetsuna), Yedo suffered (1657) from one of those immense conflagrations which were called "Yedo's flower," because, not only in this case, but in all other instances, she emerged, phoenix-like and more beautiful, from her own ashes. Iyetsuna was a patron of literature and had Hayashi, a great savant, compose an immense historical work. This was also the time when Mito was the center of learning and literature under the inspiration of its famous Prince Mitsukuni, or Gikō, who, with the aid of both Japanese and Chinese scholars, compiled the Dai Nihon Shi, which "stands at the head of Japanese histories." And from 1642 to 1662 was the period of Koxinga's supremacy in Formosa. Moreover, it was in 1666 that Louis XIV of France prepared a letter to the Emperor of Japan to ask for the French East India Company the privileges of trade in Japan, but this letter, for some reason or other, was not sent. And in 1673 the English East India Company made one more vain attempt to renew trade with Japan.[2]

The Fifth Shōgun, Tsunayoshi (1680-1709), also largely "contributed to the spread of literary pursuits." He is the one

---

[1] Dillon, *The Arts of Japan*.

[2] See Clement's Hildreth, *Japan as It Was and Is*, I, 266, 267; II, 364 f.

who "built in Yedo, and liberally endowed, a temple dedicated to Confucius"; and he is also the one who gave frequent audience to the great Dutch scholar Kaempfer, and is even said to have "facilitated his acquisition of the knowledge" of Japan and the Japanese. In his time, too, occurred the vendetta of the Forty-seven Rōnins (1701, 1702)[1] and the last eruption of Mount Fuji (1707). His reign was a glorious period for dogs, because he, having been born in a "dog year," ordered canines to be regarded as sacred animals. "A higher degree of protection was afforded to them while he lived than was given to human beings, and injuries to them were punished by more severe penalties."[2]

Just about half of Tsunayoshi's administration was taken up by the famous Genroku Era (1688-1703), which has been "compared to the Age of Pericles, the days of Louis XV, and the Venetian prime." It was the "heyday of Japanese art and culture." "There were masters in every branch of art... Pottery was represented by Ninsei and Kenzan, architecture by the great Zingoro [Jingoro], sculpture by Ritsuō, and the metallurgic art by Sōmin." Ninsei and Kenzan, as well as Hōzen and "most of the great names in Japanese Keramics, were associated with the Kyōto factories." Ritsuō is also called by Hartmann "the most skilful lacquerer the world has ever known," but Dick says that "the greatest of all names in lacquer is that of Ogata Kōrin," who, "as a lacquerer, stands alone." Hartmann acknowledges that he "achieved great triumphs as a lacquerer," but is "best known as a painter," and he calls Kōrin "the great genius of the period." Dick also characterizes him as "perhaps the greatest decorative artist Japan has produced." Both proved the truth of Gonse's statement that "Japanese lacquered objects are the most perfect works that have issued from man's hands."

---

[1] Dramatized as *Chiushingura*.

[2] Longford, *Story of Old Japan*, pp. 304-6.

In painting there are several names worthy of mention. If we take them up somewhat in chronological order, and go back to almost the beginning of this period, we have first Tanyu, "a very Japanese Whistler," "one of the greatest masters of the Kano School." His masterpiece is the four lions painted in Chinese ink on wooden panels in one of the temples at Nikkō. Later came "one of the most striking personalities among Japanese painters – Hanabusa Itchō, the last of the great Kano painters." The Tosa School was represented by Mitsuoki, "the greatest flower painter Japan has produced." It was likewise in the first half of the century that Iwasa Matahei began to represent the scenes of everyday life, and, according to Dick, founded the Ukiyoye School, which soon became popular. And Kōrin, already mentioned, has been characterized as "one of the most individual of all Japanese artists," and "the most personal of painters – the most Japanese of the Japanese."

In literature[1] we find first the name of Kaibara, who was a voluminous and valuable writer, and is perhaps best known by the *Onna Daigaku,* or "Great Learning for Women." There is also Bashō, the famous maker of "epigrams," which, in his case, translates the Japanese word *haikai.* This is a kind of poem of only seventeen syllables, arranged in three phrases in three lines of five, seven, and five syllables respectively. Such a poem certainly reaches the "extreme limit of brevity and conciseness," as well as of suggestiveness. In this era, too, Chikamatsu, who has been called "the Shakespeare of Japan," was having his plays performed in Yedo. Aston says that he is "unquestionably the most prominent figure in the history of the Japanese drama." His most famous play portrays Koxinga, the Chinese pirate mentioned above (p. 86).

While the Genroku Era was a time of great splendor,

---

[1] Aston, *History of Japanese Literature.*

magnificence, and glory, it was also an "age of abuses," of extravagance, and of dissipation. But the next two Shōguns, Iyenobu and Iyetsugu, having the assistance of the scholar and statesman, Arai Hakuseki,[1] succeeded in effecting reforms. It was at this time that a Catholic priest named Sidotti made an attempt to enter Japan in disguise, for missionary labors, but was arrested and sent to Yedo, where he was kept in confinement and finally died. With Sidotti, Arai had interesting interviews, and afterward wrote out his impressions of Western civilization, even of Christianity.

Yoshimune, the Eighth Shōgun (1716-1745), also so efficiently carried on the administration that the Kyōhō Era (1716-1736) is known as an "age of reforms," and it is very common to find references to "the peace of the Kyōhō Era." His policy in developing agriculture was so successful, and rice consequently became so cheap, that he has been dubbed "the Rice-Shōgun." And he was the one who "repealed the law which forbade the importation of books," so that both "Dutch and Chinese books were permitted to be brought in." He also encouraged the revival of the Japanese classical literature. He was himself a student of astronomy and invented astronomical instruments. Thus "the astute and comprehensive reforms of Yoshimune, followed by the prudent rule of his son Iyeshige, carried the administration of the Shōgunate to its acme of efficiency."

On the other hand, the administration of Iyeharu (1760-1786) was marked by calamity and corruption. The former included conflagrations in Yedo in 1760 and 1771, a hurricane, and a pestilence, an eruption of Mount Asama (1782), and a famine (1783), which "reduced the people to such extremities

---

[1] Aston calls Arai "the most distinguished of the Kangakusha [Chinese scholars]."

that they subsisted on dogs, cats, rats, herbs, roots, and bark," and by which more than a million people are said to have perished.

As the next Shōgun, Iyenari, was a minor, the Regent, Matsudaira, "a man of great wisdom and wide erudition," succeeded in bringing about another reform with the aid of many other able officials. And when the Shōgun attained his majority, he also proved very capable and fortunately held office for fifty years. Many feudal barons, too, like Uyesugi of Yonezawa, were distinguished for administrative ability. Moreover, there was at this time an emperor, Kōkaku, whose name is worth mentioning, because he was "a sovereign of great sagacity." Therefore, "the age is generally spoken of as that of the wise Emperor in the West [Kiōto] and of the clever Treasurer in the East [Yedo]." The closing years of the eighteenth century are known in Japan as "the Kwansei Peace," from the era which extended from 1789 to 1800, which were far from peaceful years in Europe. It was toward the close of the eighteenth century, during the long reign of Kōkaku (1779-1817) and the long administration of Iyenari (1787-1837), that efforts began to be actively made again to open communication between Japan and the outside. And it is, perhaps, not strange that the initiative was taken by Japan's nearest neighbor, Russia. In 1792, Lieutenant Laxman was sent out from Okhotsk to return some shipwrecked Japanese, and reached Hakodate and Matsumae, but was "dismissed with presents and an ample supply of provisions." The Resanoff embassy of 1804 and 1805 was a failure; and Captain Golownin and a small party, while surveying the Kurile Islands, were captured by the Russians and imprisoned in Hakodate and Matsumae for over two years (1811-1813). In 1818, Captain Gordon of the British navy entered Yedo Bay in a small brig and attempted, but in vain, to get a cargo of goods.[1]

But it may be well, now, to turn our attention to the art and literature of the eighteenth and the earlier portion of the nineteenth century. There are three writers who lived at different times during this period; but they must be mentioned together, because they constitute the glorious triumvirate of scholars who worked in apostolic succession along the same lines. These are Mabuchi (1697-1769), Motoöri (1730-1801), and Hirata (1776-1843), whose aim was to restore the Japanese language and literature to the prominent place usurped by the Chinese language, literature, and philosophy. Another phase of this movement was the revival of pure Shintō. And in the line of historical literature they had as allies, not only the standard history Dai Nihon Shi, already mentioned, but also Rai Sanyō famous *Nihon Gwaishi*, which appeared about 1837(?). All preached Nationalism and Imperialism.

It was in the latter part of the period under consideration that Japanese romance attained distinction. "The first to give to the [Japanese] world the romantic novel pure and simple" was *Kiōden* (1761-1816), whose masterpiece, according to Aston, is *Inadzuma Hiōshi*. The most famous novelist, however, and in the general estimation of the Japanese their greatest, is Bakin, who has been called "the Scott of Japan." The most famous of his novels, even of all Japanese novels, is *Hakkenden*, an enormous work of 3,000 pages, devoted to the "Story of Eight Dogs." Some Japanese critics have suggested that it should be classed among epic poems. Another novelist worthy of mention is Ikku, who was notorious on account of his eccentricities and Bohemian habits. His masterpiece is *Hizakurige*, a humorous novel like *Pickwick Papers*, giving realistic pictures of the life of his time.

The list of eighteenth-century painters starts with Ōkyo,

---

[1] See Clement's Hildreth, *Japan as It Was and Is*, chaps. xlii-xliv.

"sometimes regarded as the founder of the Shijō, or naturalistic, School." The now method, "instead of endeavoring to interpret Nature, endeavored to so present Nature that she should deliver her own message." The same school later turned out Sosen, "the greatest animal painter of Japan," "the Japanese Landseer," and "one of the world's greatest animal painters."

An outgrowth of this "natural" school of painting was the art of color printing with woodcuts,[1] by which many artists displayed their talents. "It was during a period of about half a century, say between 1760 and 1810, that the finest work was turned out." A few of these artists should be mentioned. "Kiyonaga led the Ukiyoye to greater height of technical perfection than it had ever reached before." Utamaro has been called "the greatest painter of Japanese women," and unfortunately "fell into a Bohemian way of life among the actors and courtesans who served as his models." Shunsho, Toyokuni, and Kunisada may be only named. Hiroshige, who is "generally regarded as the foremost landscape painter of Japan," carries us along to the end of the period under consideration. Mention might also be made of the Ōsaka School, which from 1820 to 1860 produced prints "with curious and well-defined characteristics."

Hokusai well deserves a paragraph by himself.[2] In Japan, critics place him only in the second rank of artists on account of "the vulgarity of his subjects" and his "mere juggling with colors." But European critics consider him "the greatest of Japanese painters," and Whistler has called him "the greatest pictorial artist since Van Dyke." He is "the greatest exponent of the realistic school"; "he alone looked out upon life with an unfettered eye, and sought to render faithfully what he saw

---

[1] See Strange, *Colour Prints of Japan.*

[2] See Strange, *Hokusai.*

therein." His works are voluminous, and the best known are *Mangwa*, "wonderful encyclopedia of Japanese life and art"; "Thirty-six [and Hundred] Views of Fuji"; "Waterfalls"; "Famous Bridges"; "Tōkaidō"; and "Twelve Scenes from the *Chiushingura.*" The two series of views of Fuji have been characterized as "a splendid epic, instinct with poetry and beauty and romance and yet filled to the full with the keenest and most kindly humanity." His *Mangwa* "covers the whole ground of Japanese life and legend, art and handicraft." On his deathbed he said: "If Heaven had lent me but five years more, I should have become a true painter"; but he did not need more time. He sometimes signed his productions with the appellation, "Old Man Mad with Painting"; and his epitaph reads: "Here lies Hokusai, a famous artist – honest and true."

Brinkley[1] says that "the Tokugawa Era (1620-1850) is justly regarded as the golden period of the bronze caster's art," and was marked "by a long series of beautiful works executed for the mausolea of the Tokugawa in Yedo and Nikkō, and for other temples and shrines throughout the Empire." This same period, Dick[2] says, "especially in its earlier stages, is pre-eminently the period of the minor arts, which then reached a perfection which has not been attained before or since." This may be illustrated by only one example, that of the *netsuke,* the carver of which Dick calls "the greatest master of the art of *multum in parvo* that the world has seen."

During all this period under consideration, the Dutch, who were the only persons allowed to carry on trade with Japan, were the only means of communication with the outside world. Thus it was through them that the Japanese and other nations gained knowledge of each other, and, in spite of official restrictions,

---

[1] *Japan; Its History, Arts and Literature*, Vol. VII.

[2] *The Arts and Crafts of Old Japan.*

succeeded in learning a great deal from each other. We are indebted to men like Caron, Kaempfer, Thunberg, Titsingh, von Siebold, and others for pictures of Japanese life.[1] And the Japanese were likewise indebted to such men for important knowledge, especially scientific, obtained at first secretly and at risk of life, but none the less influencing Japanese thought.[2] The Dutch certainly helped make Modern Japan.

Inasmuch as the Chinese influences were so powerful in literary circles during this period, it is not strange that Confucianism was the prevailing philosophy (mental and moral) of the time. It is true that Japanese Confucianism was quite different in many respects from Chinese Confucianism. Japanese scholars at first followed the school of Chu Hi, known in Japan as Shushi; but afterward many of them adopted the Ōyōmei doctrines; and these they always modified to suit the Japanese needs. The chief Chinese scholars were Arai, Kiusō, and several generations of the Hayashi family. Among the military class, the usual eclecticism succeeded in evolving from Shintō, Confucianism, and Buddhism a syncretic system known as Bushidō ("The Way of the Warrior"), which made the Japanese knight *(samurai)* a peculiar type and most profoundly influenced Japanese character.[3] As Murdoch points out, feudal Japan produced "no Pascal, no Newton, no Leibnitz, and no Watt"; but she produced a Ninomiya Sontoku, ethical economist.[4]

The Twelfth Tokugawa Shōgun was Iyeyoshi (1837- 1853). It was in 1837 that the "Morrison," coming to Japan without armament of any kind, but on an errand of mercy to return shipwrecked Japanese, was fired on in both Yedo and Kagoshima

---

[1] See Clement's Hildreth, *Japan as It Was and Is.*

[2] See Griffs, *Japan in History, Folk-Lore and Art*, chap. xxiii, and Mitsukuri's paper in *Transactions of the Asiatic Society of Japan*, Vol. V.

[3] See Nitobe, *Bushido.*

[4] See Armstrong, *Just before the Dawn.*

bays. In 1844, William II of Holland sent a letter to recommend the opening of Japan to foreign trade. Two years later Commodore Biddle carried a friendly letter from President Polk for the Emperor; and his purpose was "to ascertain whether the ports of Japan were accessible"; but he was asked to depart immediately. In 1848, the "Ladoga," an American whaler, was wrecked off Matsumae in the island of Yezo; and the survivors were kept in confinement, first in Matsumae and afterward in Nagasaki. In 1849, they were released and taken away by Commander Glynn in the "Preble."[1]

In the closing days of Iyeyoshi's administration Japan, especially Yedo, was stirred by an event of which probably few, if any, realized the full significance. On July 7, 1853, Commodore Perry[2] with his "black ships" "sailed into the Sea of Sagami and into Japanese history," and dropped anchor off Uraga. As a Japanese writer has expressed it, "the American fleet stole into the quiet waters of Yedo Bay, which had never before been plowed by a Western vessel, and amid the roaring of cannon, loudly knocked at the door of Uraga to awaken us from our long sleep." Perry was, as usual, ordered to go to Nagasaki, and, not as usual, declined to obey. He insisted that he would stay there and deliver the letter and the presents from President Fillmore to the Emperor. On the following Sunday the American fleet strictly refused to receive visitors and observed the Sabbath. For the first time in modern days in Japan the strains of a Christian hymn were heard. Meanwhile the authorities at Yedo were discussing the course to be pursued with this persistent and patient "barbarian." They finally decided to receive the letter in order to get rid of the troublesome visitor, and only hoped that this would end the matter. Therefore, on July 14, 1853, the accredited

---

[1] For details of these events, see Clement's Hildreth, *Japan as It Was and Is.*

[2] See Griffis, *Matthew Calbraith Perry.*

representatives of the Shōgun, a pavilion specially erected for the purpose at Kurihama, near Uraga, formally received from the accredited representative of the United States government a letter from the President to the Emperor. This was done, as stated in the official receipt for the letter, "in opposition to Japanese law." Thus, when the Japanese authorities broke their own laws, the downfall of the old system was inevitable. This act was a clear confession that the old policy of seclusion and its prohibitions could no longer be strictly maintained. Japan awoke from sleep; Old Japan received its death-warrant; and New Japan was born on July 14, 1853.

CHAPTER XI. TOKUGAWA FEUDALISM, III

Awakening of Japan (1853-1868)

a) *Treaty-making* (1853-1858). – As already stated in the previous chapter, July 14, 1853, was the real birthday of New Japan, because the receipt on that day of a letter from the President of the United States of America by representatives of the Shōgun, in whom was vested the administration of affairs, in opposition to the old law absolutely forbidding all communication with foreign nations except through the Dutch at Nagasaki, sounded the death knell of the old régime of seclusion. It was truly the beginning of the end of Old Japan. Of course, the Japanese authorities expected that the matter would end there and that they would be able in some way to evade the necessity for a reply to the letter from President Fillmore. Soon after Perry had left, with the assurance that he would return the next spring for the answer to the letter, "the Shōgun Iyeyoshi, who had been ill since the beginning of the summer, was rendered very anxious about this sudden and pressing affair of the outer barbarians" and died.

The new Shōgun, Iyesada, at first influenced by the old Prince of Mito, began to make preparations for a warlike reception; but afterward impelled, partly by other counsels, and partly by the impossibility of making the military preparations efficient in time, decided to receive the Americans "peaceably." He therefore appointed one Hayashi, a good Chinese and Confucian scholar, with the title of "Regent of the University" *(Daigaku no Kami),* to treat with Commodore Perry, who returned in February, 1854. It is scarcely worth while to go into the details[1] of the negotiations; it is sufficient to state here that

---

[1] See Griffis, *Matthew Calbraith Perry,* and the official account of "Perry's Expedition to Japan."

on March 31, 1854, a treaty of peace and amity was signed at Kanagawa (Yokohama). As this was the first treaty made by Japan in modern times with a foreign nation, the following synopsis[1] may be interesting:

I. Peace and friendship.

II. Ports of Shimoda and Hakodate open to American ships, and necessary provisions to be supplied them.

III. Relief to shipwrecked people; expenses thereof not to be refunded.

IV. Americans to be free as in other countries, but amenable to just laws.

V. Americans at Shimoda and Hakodate not to be subject to restrictions; free to go about within defined limits.

VI. Careful deliberation in transacting business which affects the welfare of either party.

VII. Trade in open ports subject to local regulations.

VIII. Wood, water, provisions, coal, etc., to be procured through Japanese officers only.

IX. Most-favored nation clause.

X. United States ships restricted to ports of Shimoda and Hakodate, except when forced by stress of weather.

XI. United States consuls or agents to reside at Shimoda.

XII. Ratifications to be exchanged within eighteen months.

After that it was no difficult matter, of course, for other nations to obtain the same privileges; so that similar treaties were signed as follows: British, October 15, 1854; Russian, February 7, 1855; and Dutch, January 30, 1856.

It goes without saying that these treaties produced a great commotion in Japan. "It was charged against the Shōgun that, in making treaties with foreign nations, he had transcended the

---

[1] From Nitobe, *Intercourse between the United States and Japan.*

power that rightly belonged to him. He was not the sovereign of Japan and never had been. He was only the chief executive under the Emperor." And such facts as that Yedo was visited in 1855 by a terrible earthquake, followed by an immense conflagration, in which 100,000 people are said to have lost their lives; that the eastern section of the Empire was devastated by a storm in the same year; and that the annals of the years 1854 to 1856 record pestilence, floods, fires, earthquakes, wind-storms, etc., in various localities – all these were both single and cumulative evidences that the Japanese gods were wroth and were visiting the nation with such calamities by way of punishment for breaking the laws and traditions of the Empire.

But a very important figure appeared on the scene in the person of Townsend Harris. He had been appointed United States Consul-General to Japan in 1855 and arrived at Shimoda in August, 1856. There, on September 4, he hoisted the "first consular flag ever seen in this Empire"; and, having carried the American flag from Shimoda to Yedo, on November 30 entered the Shōgun's capital as the "first diplomatic representative that has ever been received in this city"; and on December 7 was received in audience by the Shōgun – the first foreign representative to be so honored. Then followed several months of tedious and trying formal negotiations for a new treaty, the details of which[1] are not uninteresting, but need not be given here.

One can now, from the better knowledge of Japanese history than Townsend Harris possessed, sympathize a little with the Japanese in their dilemma, due to complications of national politics; but we must also feel glad that the negotiator on the other side was a man who had patience, perseverance, common-sense, tact, and honesty. The fine tribute by the British official

---

[1] See Griffis, *Townsend Harris.*

and historian Longford[1] is worth quoting, as follows:

> *The story of how, unbacked by any display of force*
> *under his country's flag, he succeeded by his own*
> *personal efforts in overcoming the traditional hatred*
> *of centuries to even the smallest association with*
> *foreigners, is one of marvellous tact and patience, of*
> *steady determination and courage, of*
> *straightforward uprightness in every respect, that is*
> *not exceeded by any in the entire history of the*
> *international relations of the world. He won the*
> *confidence and trust of the Japanese.*

Much to the surprise of Mr. Harris, the only article of his draft which was at once accepted was that which called for the abolition of the practice of trampling on the cross and gave Americans the free exercise of their religion. On the other hand, the article upon which it was most difficult to come to an agreement was that relating to the opening of new ports and other cities.

Finally, however, both sides succeeded in agreeing upon the terms of a treaty of amity and commerce, which was signed July 29, 1858, to go into effect July 4, 1859, and was, therefore, in force forty full years – till July, 1899. This treaty was followed by treaties, on similar terms, with Great Britain, Russia, France, Holland, Prussia, Switzerland, Italy, Belgium, Austria-Hungary, Spain, Denmark, Hawaii, Sweden and Norway, Portugal, and Peru, which countries, together with the United States of America, constituted what were known as the sixteen "treaty-powers."

b) *Civil commotions* (1858-1868). – Again at a critical period in Japanese history (1858), the Shōgun (Iyesada) died, [2]and was

---

[1] See *Story of Old Japan*, p. 302.

[2] Possibly of cholera, then raging.

succeeded by his son, Iyemochi, who was only twelve years of age. Thus the real power and authority were in the hands of his Chief Minister *(Tairō)*, Ii Kamon-no-Kami, who had had the audacity to cause the Shōgun to sign the treaties without waiting for the Emperor's sanction. In 1859, Kanagawa (or Yokohama) (in place of Shimoda, destroyed by an earthquake), Nagasaki, and Hakodate were opened to foreign trade, and began at once to become populous and prosperous. In the same year Harris was promoted to the position of Minister, and (Sir) Rutherford Alcock arrived as the first British Minister. This was a red-letter year, not only for merchants but also for missionaries. Roman Catholic priests, who had been waiting in the Riūkiū Islands for the opportunity now afforded by the treaty with France, at once came to Nagasaki to reopen their work, after the long interval of two hundred and fifty years. The first Protestant missionaries, Liggins and Williams (American Episcopal), Verbeck, Brown, and Simmons (Dutch Reformed), and Hepburn (American Presbyterian), arrived in the spring and fall of the same year. And in 1860 came Jonathan Goble (Baptist), who had been a sailor with Perry: he was to win greater fame as inventor of the *jinrikisha.*

Early in 1860 the Shōgun sent envoys to the United States of America to confirm the treaty. In the same year occurred what is known as the "Sakurada affair," because it took place just outside the Sakurada Gate of the Shōgun's, now the imperial, palace. The Shōgun's Minister, Ii, had stirred up so much enmity against him on the part of those who were in favor of driving out the "barbarians" instead of opening the country, that he was marked for assassination. Finally, a band of Rōnin,[1] chiefly old Mito retainers, succeeded in carrying out their purpose in the midst of a snowstorm on March 24. This event gave some impetus to the

---

[1] Unattached knights.

"anti-foreign" movement, and frequent attacks on foreigners followed. In 1861, Mr. Heusken, the first interpreter of the United States legation, was assassinated, and the British legation was attacked by Mito Rōnin. The Shōgun's government really seemed to be too weak to prevent such outrages. Thereupon all the foreign representatives, except Harris, left Yedo for Yokohama, where they remained a few weeks, but returned when they were assured of protection.

The following year (1862) was marked by three important events. One was the dispatch of an embassy to America and Europe to ask for a postponement of the dates for the opening of Hyōgo and Niigata and the establishment of "foreign concessions" in Yedo and Osaka. It succeeded in securing a postponement for five years – to January 1, 1868.[1]

Another event was the "Richardson affair," which, though apparently trivial, produced tremendous results. Richardson was an Englishman who, with two other gentlemen and one lady, was out on a ride from Yokohama to Kawasaki on September 14. A little beyond Kanagawa they met the feudal train of the Prince of Satsuma and in some way or other failed to satisfy the demands of Japanese etiquette on such occasions. Thereupon the Satsuma *samurai* attacked the party, killed Richardson, and wounded the two other gentlemen. The British immediately demanded the punishment of the assassin of Richardson and indemnities from both the Shōgunate and the Prince of Satsuma.[2] When the latter failed to respond to these demands, a British squadron was dispatched to Kiūshiu, and bombarded Kagoshima till it was "almost completely destroyed by fire."

In that same year (1862), American, French, and Dutch ships, passing through the Straits of Shimonoseki, were fired

---

[1] This embassy was an eye-opener both to Japanese and Westerners.

[2] From the Shōgunate £100,000 and from Satsuma £3,000.

upon by the shore batteries which the Prince of Chōshiu had erected on his own territory. American and French vessels were at once dispatched, by which these batteries were silenced. And later, when negotiations for damages failed to accomplish anything, an expedition was organized under British, Dutch, French, and American auspices, to bombard Shimonoseki. After an attack of several days, the Prince "gave in his absolute submission." A convention was held later, by which Japan was forced to pay an indemnity of $3,000,000 to the four powers. The language of Murray[1] concerning this "dollar diplomacy" seems scarcely too strong: "It has always been felt that the exaction of this large indemnity was a harsh if not unwarrantable proceeding." But it remains to the everlasting credit of the United States that, in 1883, her full share of that indemnity was returned to Japan for use in educational work.

It was also in the year 1864 that Rev. J. H. Ballagh had the honor of administering the first baptism to a Japanese convert in Japan proper in the person of Yano Riyu. It is, however, possible that an earlier convert was Wakasa-no-Kami, who was not baptized till 1866.

Meanwhile, the internal affairs of Japan had been getting into greater and greater confusion, of which Kyōto became the center. The Chōshiu clansmen were expelled from Kyōto, and in 1864 made a vain attempt to get back into the capital. Through the intervention of Satsuma, which had itself become reconciled with Chōshiu, peace was made between the latter and the Shōgun.

Then the representatives of the foreign powers, under the leadership of (Sir) Harry Parkes, the new British Minister, "made a demonstration" with their naval armaments at Hyōgo and Ōsaka, where the Shōgun was then staying, and urged upon him

---

[1] *Japan*, pp. 349, 350.

to obtain the Emperor's approval of the treaties. The Shōgun's guardian, Prince Keiki, was wise enough to recognize that the time had come to end the confusion, turmoil, and uncertainty. In reply, therefore, to a memorial from the Shōgun, the Emperor gave his formal sanction to the treaties and to a tariff convention (1865).

This is also the year when the new Roman Catholic cathedral[1] at Nagasaki was dedicated to the memory of the twenty-six martyrs who had suffered death in that city in 1597. Within less than a month, on St. Patrick's Day, March 17, occurred the wonderful scene which is known as "The Finding of the Christians," or the discovery of thousands of Catholics who had "kept the faith" handed down during the centuries.

In 1866 came the third instance of a Shōgun's death at a critical time, and a few months later, in 1867, the Emperor Kōmei died from smallpox, which the superstitious conservatives attributed to the fact that he had sanctioned the treaties. The new Shōgun was the aforementioned Keiki, son of the old Mito prince, but adopted into the Hitotsubashi family; while the new Emperor, Mutsuhito, was a youth of only fifteen years of age.

The new Shōgun had already begun to realize that the time was ripe for a radical change in the form of government and that unification of administration was necessary. He was, therefore, ready to listen to the advice of the Prince of Tosa, who, in October of 1867, presented him with a memorial and a recommendation. We quote these few sentences:

> The cause of this [situation] lies in the fact that the
> administration proceeds from two centres, causing
> the Empire's eyes and ears to be turned in two
> different directions. The march of events has brought

---

[1] One had been dedicated in 1862 in Yokohama.

about a revolution, and the old system can no longer
be persevered in. You should restore the governing
power into the hands of the sovereign, and so lay a
foundation on which Japan may take its stand as the
equal of all other countries.[1]

Accordingly, on November 19, 1867, Keiki surrendered into the hands of the Emperor his authority as Shōgun; and he thus ended both the Tokugawa Dynasty and the whole Shōgunate system. All honor to Keiki, who had the vision to see, and the wisdom to recognize, that he was "the last of the Shōguns"!

But, in the reorganization of the government, early in 1868, the friends of the ex-Shōgun were dismissed, and the Satsuma and Chōshiu clans were given so much power that it looked as if the Tokugawa Shōgunate had merely been superseded by a Sat-Chō Shōgunate. The Tokugawa adherents, therefore, under the leadership of the warlike Aizu clan, persuaded the ex-Shōgun to attempt to "remove from the Emperor his bad councillors and try the issue with them by the sword." This move was met by military preparations on the part of the government at Kyōto; and in a battle at Fushimi the ex-Shōgun was defeated and retreated to his castle in Ōsaka.[2] Later he fled to Yedo, where he finally surrendered and retired, first to Mito and then to Suruga (Shizuoka). His adherents kept up the contest in fierce battles at Uyeno in Yedo, at Wakamatsu, and in the Hokkaidō, where they tried to set up a republic!

The result of all this conflict was what is called by some the "Restoration" and by others the "Revolution." Certainly from the Tokugawa point of view it was a revolution, which ended the administrative power that the family had held for 265 years in the Shōgunate. And assuredly from the imperial point of view it

---

[1] *Kinse Shiriaku* (Satow translation).

[2] This battle of Fushimi, Longford calls a "decisive battle" in the history of Japan.

was a restoration to the Emperor, the only lawful ruler, of his inherited legal authority. He now became sovereign both *de jure* and *de facto,* both in name and in fact.

"Thus at last was worked out the unification of Japan," says Lloyd,[1] who also points out that it happened eight (seven?) years after the unification of Italy and three years before the unification of Germany, and that the unification of all presented "many of the same features." As the year 1867[2] had witnessed this restoration of the Emperor to his full authority, the next year, 1868, was made the first of a new era, called Meiji, or "Enlightened Rule."

---

[1] *Every Day Japan*, p. 364.

[2] The third year of the Keiō Era, from which Mr. Fukuzawa's school, the Keiō-gijiku (now a university), in Tōkyō, derived its name.

CHAPTER XII. THE MEIJI ERA, I

1868-1912

The two names, Mutsuhito and Meiji, are practically synonymous. Mutsuhito is the personal name of the late Emperor, who succeeded to the throne upon the death of the Emperor Kōmei in 1867, but was not formally crowned until 1868. Meiji is the name of the year-period, or era, which began with 1868 and ended with the death of Mutsuhito in 1912. Although, therefore, it may not be absolutely accurate from the mathematical point of view to write "Mutsuhito = Meiji," yet the two terms are practically equivalent and synchronous. The reign of Mutsuhito was the Enlightened Rule of Meiji. And it is the longest reign in all the authentic history of Japan. As the incredibly long lives and reigns of the earliest emperors (before 400 A.D.) cannot be accepted on account of the unreliable chronology, the forty-five years' reign of Mutsuhito holds the record.

It is possible to dismiss in one paragraph the important points of the purely individual biography of the late Emperor as follows:

Mutsuhito was born, the only son of the Emperor Kōmei, on November 3, 1852; was proclaimed Crown Prince on July 10, 1860; succeeded to the throne on the death of his father in January, 1867, but was not formally crowned till October 31, 1868; was married in Kyōto, early in 1869, to Haru-Ko, daughter of Prince Ichijō; became the father of three sons and nine daughters, of whom one son (the present Emperor) and three daughters survive; in 1894 publicly celebrated his silver wedding anniversary; and died July 30, 1912, at the age of sixty-one by Japanese count and of almost sixty by Occidental reckoning. And now, if the important public events of the reign of the late

Emperor are treated in connection with the Meiji Era, it seems proper to subdivide that epoch into five periods:

> 1. *Reconstruction (1868-1878).*
>
> 2. *Internal Development (1879-1889).*
>
> 3. *Constitutionalism (1889-1899).*
>
> 4. *Cosmopolitanism (1899-1910).*
>
> 5. *Continentalism (1910 –).*

It should, however, be clearly understood that these distinctions are not absolute, but rather relative. And yet it is possible, by the names of these periods, to trace the general progress that marked the Meiji Era.

1. *Reconstruction* (1868-1878). – It was on January 1, 1868, that Hyōgo (Kōbe) and Osaka were opened to foreign trade; and in the following year, when Yedo and Niigata were opened, the obligations of the treaty in that respect were completely fulfilled.

On February 3, 1868, the Emperor issued to the foreign representatives the following manifesto:

> *The Emperor of Japan announces to the sovereigns of all foreign nations and to their subjects, that permission has been granted to the Shōgun Yoshinobu to return the governing power in accordance with his own request. Henceforward we shall exercise supreme authority both in the internal and external affairs of the country. Consequently the title of Emperor should be substituted for that of Tycoon [Taikun], which has been hitherto employed in the treaties. Officers are being appointed by us to conduct foreign affairs. It is desirable that the represen-tatives of all the treaty powers should recognize this announcement.*[1]

---

[1] Adams, *History of Japan*, II, 105.

Of this manifesto one writer says: "Appended were the seal of Dai Nippon, and the signature, Mutsuhito, this being the first occasion in Japanese history on which the name of an Emperor had appeared during his lifetime."[1]

The Emperor also invited the foreign representatives to an audience before him in Kyōto on March 23. "The significance of this event can scarcely now be conceived. Never before in the history of the Empire had its divine head deigned to admit to his presence the despised foreigner, or put himself on an equality with the sovereign of the foreigner."[2] The audiences of the French and Dutch Ministers proceeded without any serious incident; but, when the British Minister, Parkes, was on his way, his escort was suddenly attacked by two *samurai,* who wounded nine of them before one of the *samurai* was killed and the other wounded and captured. The party had to return to their lodgings; but the interrupted audience was held on the 26th. The captured assailant was afterward condemned to death by *harakiri.*[3]

In 1868 the name of Yedo was altered to Tōkyō, which means "Eastern Capital," and Kyōto was renamed Saikyō, or "Western Capital"; but the new name of the latter has not supplanted the old name, as has happened in the case of Tōkyō. This transfer of title has been accompanied by an actual transfer of influence; so that it is most appropriate for Aston to call the Meiji Era in Japanese literature the "Tōkyō Period." It may also be called the "Period of Western Influence," not merely in literature but in almost all phases of civilization. In 1869 the young Emperor returned to Kyōto for a short visit, during which he was married to Princess Haru of the Ichijō family. In the spring of that year

---

[1] Dixon, *Land of the Morning,* p. 97.

[2] Murray, *Japan,* p. 373.

[3] For a good description of the formal ceremony of *harakiri,* see Mitford, *Tales of Old Japan,* Appendix.

the Emperor took his' famous "Charter Oath" to the following effect, as summarized by Iyenaga:

> *1. A deliberative assembly should be formed, and all measures be decided by public opinion.*
> *2. The principles of social and political economics should be diligently studied by both the superior and [the] inferior classes of our people.*
> *3. Everyone in the community shall be assisted to persevere in carrying out his will for good purposes.*
> *4. All the old absurd usages of former times should be disregarded, and the impartiality and justice displayed in the workings of nature be adopted as a basis of action.*
> *5. Wisdom and ability should be sought after in all quarters of the world for the purpose of firmly establishing the foundations of the Empire.*[1]

Meantime, a memorial signed first by the most wealthy and influential, and afterward by almost all of the *daimyō,* had been presented to the Emperor, to whom at the same time were offered all their fiefs. We quote a part, as follows:

> *The place where we live is the Emperor's land, and the food which we eat is grown by the Emperor's men. How can we make it our own? We now reverently offer up the list of our possessions and men, with the prayer that the Emperor will take good measures for rewarding those to whom reward is due, and for taking from those to whom punishment is due. Let the Imperial orders be issued for altering and remodeling the territories of the various clans.*[2]

This "revolution" was not completely carried out till 1871,

---

[1] *Constitutional Development of Japan.*

[2] Adams, *History of Japan,* II, 181, 182.

when feudalism was abolished by the following laconic decree: "The clans *[han]* are abolished, and prefectures *[ken]* are established in their places."

The financial problem in connection with the abolition of the fiefs was a most difficult and troublesome one. It was finally decided that a dispossessed prince should receive one-tenth of the amount of his former income, and that the *samurai* (retainers) should receive varying lump sums according to circumstances. To accomplish this, the government borrowed $165,000,000, which had to be added to the public debt.

It was also in 1869 that the first single lady missionary arrived in the person of Miss Mary Kidder,[1] of the Dutch Reformed Mission; and it was in 1871 that Nicolai, who had first come to Japan ten years previous as chaplain to the Russian consulate in Hakodate, came to Tōkyō and began mission work for the Greek, or Russian, Church.

This was naturally the great period of "firsts," of beginnings, along new lines. When Perry came to Japan he brought with him a great many presents, which were object-lessons of the accomplishments of Western civilization. These gifts to the "Emperor" included the electric telegraph, the steam locomotive and train, the telescope, life-boats, stoves, clocks, sewing-machines, agricultural implements and machinery, standard scales, weights, measures, maps and charts, etc.[2]

One of the first purposes of the reorganized government was the improvement of means of communication. Along this line the process of reconstruction called for something more rapid than the old-style *kago* and *norimono,* or even the new-style *jinrikisha* and carriage drawn by horsepower. As a result, in 1870 the first line of telegraph was set up between Yokohama and

---

[1] The late Mrs. E. R. Miller, of Tōkyō.

[2] See Griffis, *Matthew Calbraith Perry.* p. 368.

Tōkyō; and in 1872 the first line of railway (narrow-gauge of 3 feet 6 inches) was opened to cover the 18 miles between those two cities. Lighthouses had also been erected in 1870 to render safer and more easily accessible the coast of the country which had for so long a period excluded foreign shipping. In the following year the government established a modern postal system, to which was added, in 1872, a foreign postal service. And from time to time were added all the modern conveniences to accommodate the people; so that the Japanese enjoyed universal free delivery, postal savings banks, and a parcels post long before the United States.

It was likewise in 1872 that Black's *Nisshin Shinjishi,* which Chamberlain calls "the first newspaper worthy of the name" in Japan, was started in Yokohama. It is, however, only fair to "Joseph Heco," a naturalized American citizen, to state that he claims that honor for his *Kaigai Shimbun* of 1864 to 1865. He was a Japanese who, having been rescued from shipwreck, was carried to America in 1850, but returned to Japan in 1859.[1]

Among other interesting "firsts" of this sub-period, the first audience given by the young Empress in 1873 to foreign ladies should by no means fail to be mentioned.

The first mint and the first dock (1871) should also appear in this list.

In 1872 an Educational Law was enacted in which was laid the foundation of compulsory education. Normal schools and the *Kaisei Gakkō,* which was the forerunner of the present Imperial University at Tōkyō, were established.

The first Christian church in Modern Japan was established in Yokohama in 1872.

The abolition of feudalism in 1871 had been accompanied by another great social reform in the admission of *eta* and *hinin,* or

---

[1] See his *Narrative of a Japanese.*

"the outcasts," to the rank of humanity and citizenship. They had been counted as "animals," but now they were named in the registers and enrolled among the population of Japan.

In the treaties with the great powers it was provided that the treaties might be revised at any time after July 1, 1872. It was with the purpose of inducing the powers to begin negotiations for the revision of the treaties on terms less galling to the Japanese that the Iwakura embassy was dispatched in 1871 to America and Europe. The chief ambassador was Prince Iwakura, who was Junior Prime Minister. The four associate ambassadors were Ōkubo, Minister of Finance; Kido, a Privy Councillor; Itō, Acting Minister of Public Works; and Yamaguchi, Assistant Minister of Foreign Affairs. All afterward became very prominent in the reconstruction work. They were attended by a large number of secretaries, commissioners, and officers. Their visit abroad opened their eyes to the fact that their country had not reached that degree of civilization which would warrant the powers of Christendom in admitting Japan to full standing in the comity of nations. But, though they failed in the prime purpose of the embassy, they both taught and learned most valuable lessons. Two immediate results of the embassy were seen in the removal of the anti-Christian edicts from the public bulletin-boards and the adoption of the Gregorian, or Christian, calendar, to take effect January 1, 1873.

With that embassy, five Japanese girls, the first to go abroad, went to America for study and training. Two of them had to return soon on account of ill-health, but the other three spent several years in the United States. They are now Miss Ume Tsuda, one of the leading female educators; Baroness Uriu, whose husband attended the Naval Academy at Annapolis; and Princess Oyama, wife of the famous Field Marshal. The last was a regular graduate of Vassar with honors. They are all influential "new women" in New Japan.

The members of the Iwakura embassy also came back filled with the idea that Japan needed peace, in order properly to carry on the necessary reforms. They were able to defeat the party which was urging war with Korea. This, however, led to internal disturbances, aroused by disgruntled *samurai* and conservative leaders. In 1874 a rebellion broke out in Saga Province under the leadership of Eto. This was soon quelled. Then the government determined to utilize the "fighting spirit" of the discontented by an expedition to Formosa against the savages, who had murdered some Japanese merchants. This was successful, both from a military and a financial standpoint; in the latter case, it brought an indemnity of £50,000 to Japan.

In 1877 a more serious rebellion broke out in Satsuma under the leadership of the great hero Saigō.[1] It took the government several months to overcome this outbreak at great cost of men and money. But it was the first, and a successful, test of the new national army, organized under the conscription system, which had been adopted in 1873.

The peaceful policy was strengthened by the exchange with Russia of Sakhalin for the Kurile Islands in 1875, and a treaty, instead of war, with Korea in 1876. These same two years were marked by the establishment of the Hakuaisha, which later became the Japan Red Cross Society, and by the recognition of Sunday as an official day of rest. The next two years (1877 and 1878) saw the organization of the Japan Evangelical Alliance, and of various Christian schools, as well as the ordination of Sawayama, the first case of the rite being performed in Japan. The first Japanese, however, to be ordained to the Christian ministry had been Neeshima, whose ordination took place in 1874 in Massachusetts.[2]

---

[1] See Mounsey, *Satsuma Rebellion.*

[2] See Davis, *Joseph Hardy Neeshima.*

The First National Exhibition of Japan was held in Tōkyō in 1877.

In this prolific period of "firsts," one can find, in political affairs, the first assembly of provincial governors to confer together upon general policy, and the first Senate, which later became the House of Peers. And this subperiod, the first decade of the Meiji Era, closes in 1878, when bimetallism was adopted and a promise was made to establish prefectural assemblies or training-schools in political science through practice in local self-government.

CHAPTER XIII. THE MEIJI ERA, II

2. *Internal development* (1879-1889). – This decade is not marked, perhaps, by so many striking events as the preceding one; but it was a period of somewhat quiet, though rapid, internal development. Brinkley has so well summarized the work of "progressive reform," that we do not hesitate to quote at some length, as follows:

> *They [the statesmen in power] recast the Ministry,*
> *removing the Court nobles, appointing one of the*
> *young reformers (Itō Hirobumi) to the post of*
> *Premier, and organising the departments on the lines*
> *of a European government. They rehabilitated the*
> *nobility, creating five orders – prince, marquis,*
> *count, viscount, and baron – and granting patents to*
> *the men who had taken leading parts in the*
> *Restoration. They codified the civil and penal laws,*
> *remodelling them on Western bases. They brought a*
> *vast number of affairs within the scope of minute*
> *regulations. They rescued the finances from*
> *confusion and restored them to a sound condition.*
> *They recast the whole framework of local*
> *government. They organized a great national bank*
> *and established a network of subordinate institutions*
> *throughout the country. They pushed the work of*
> *railway construction and successfully enlisted private*
> *enterprise in its cause. They steadily extended the*
> *postal and telegraphic services. They economised*
> *public expenditures so that the State's income always*
> *exceeded its outlays. They laid the foundations of a*
> *strong mercantile marine. They instituted a system of*
> *postal savings banks. They undertook large harbor*

> *improvement and road-making. They planned and*
> *put into operation an extensive programme of*
> *riparian improvement. They made civil-service*
> *appointments depend on competitive examination.*
> *They sent numbers of students to Europe and*
> *America to complete their studies; and, by tactful,*
> *persevering diplomacy, they gradually introduced a*
> *new tone into the Empire's relations with foreign*
> *Powers.*[1]

Some of these points must be explained more fully. The Cabinet, as reorganized, and as still constituted, consists of ten members, as follows: Prime Minister, Ministers of Home Affairs, Foreign Affairs, Treasury, Army, Navy, Justice, Education, Agriculture and Commerce, and Communications. There is also a Minister of the Imperial Household Department; but he has no seat in the Cabinet. A Privy Council was also established.

The people of Japan, outside of the imperial family, are divided into three classes: the nobility (mentioned above); the gentry, who are descendants of the old *samurai* class; and the common people.

The Yokohama Specie Bank was organized in 1880 for the special purpose of facilitating foreign exchange. And when the various national banks found it impossible to maintain specie payments, it was evident that there was need of a strong central bank. In 1882, therefore, the Bank of Japan was organized "for the purpose of bringing the other banks nearer together and of facilitating the monetary circulation throughout the country."[2] This is the only bank which has the power to issue convertible bank notes. This is also the period in which (in 1879) the pioneer

---

[1] *Japan*, IV, 233, 234.

[2] The Bank of Japan has ever since been a most important agent in maintaining an economic equilibrium.

clearing house, that of Ōsaka, was opened.

In the preceding period, by the encouragement of the government, private steamship companies had been organized; and two more companies were organized in 1882 and 1884. One of these is the *Ōsaka Shōsen Kaisha* (Ōsaka Mercantile Marine Company), which is still in existence and doing a flourishing business. The other company, "after a desperate competition," united with an earlier company (Mitsubishi Mail Steamship Company) and formed the well-known *Nippon Yūsen Kaisha* (Japan Mail Steamship Company), which operates several foreign lines. It has been instrumental in expanding Japanese trade and commerce.

In 1882 Count Ōkuma's well-known institution at Waseda in Tōkyō was started. English was introduced into the curriculum of Japanese schools in 1884; and the cause of Christian education was strengthened during this sub-period by the opening of several new institutions and the expansion of the Dōshisha, which had been opened in 1875 in Kyōto.

Some obstacles in the way of the progress of Christianity were removed in 1884 by the disestablishment of both Buddhism and Shintō. And great assistance to the propagation of the gospel was afforded by the completion of the translation of the Bible, that of the New Testament being finished in 1880 and of the Old Testament in 1888. The great Missionary Conference in Ōsaka in 1883 had given to the work a new impetus and had led to the first "revivals" in Japan. The visit of Mrs. Leavitt to Japan in 1880 gave great encouragement to temperance work along Christian lines and led to the formation, not only of local temperance societies, but also of a Woman's Christian Temperance Union, which has been a great power for social purity and for righteousness. In 1887 the late Mr. Ishii, "the George Müller of Japan," founded the Okayama Orphan Asylum, which is now the largest and best known of such institutions.

This period was called, at the outset, one of "somewhat *quiet*" internal development. It was filled, however, with what Chamberlain, in his *Things Japanese,* dubs "Fashionable Crazes." In 1882 and 1883 the craze was printing dictionaries and other works by subscription; and this was the great time for founding societies, learned and otherwise. In 1884 and 1885 the people took up athletics; and in 1886 and 1887 waltzing was the rage. This was also about the time when "the German measles" prevailed; but it was only a mania for imitating "things German." In 1888 mesmerism, table-turning, planchette, and wrestling were fashionable. In 1889 there was a general revival of "things Japanese," so that this has been called "the great year of reaction."

The status of the Riūkiū Islands was settled during this period. The people of that country had tried to maintain friendly relations with both China and Japan, and, calling the former "father" and the latter "mother," had sent tribute to both. In 1868 the King of Riūkiū had acknowledged the new Emperor as his suzerain; in 1879 he was made a noble of Japan, and Riūkiū was formally annexed. The year before, Japan had formally annexed the Bonin Islands.

In 1882 a Korean mob attacked the Japanese legation at Seoul and burned it. The Minister and his staff made their escape with great difficulty. The result was that, in 1885, a treaty between Japan and China recognized the right of both nations to station troops in Korea, especially in Seoul.

The subject of treaty revision was a lively one during this decade. It was brought up before the treaty powers in 1882 by Inouye; and the principal point in the terms suggested was that a certain number of foreign judges should be appointed for a certain number of years, and that they should form a majority in all cases affecting foreigners. It is scarcely profitable to enter very minutely on the tedious details of that subject and of the prolonged discussions which ensued. Suffice it to say that the demands made by the foreign representatives and almost accepted by Count Inouye were so humiliating to the national dignity, and caused such a strong hostility in the public mind, that Count Inouye was compelled to postpone the negotiations and resigded his portfolio. He was succeeded in the Foreign Office by Count Ōkuma, who, with modified conditions,[1] began negotiations with the powers one by one, and had succeeded with the United States, Germany, Russia, and France, when public opinion again asserted its power in opposition and drove Count Ōkuma also out of office, after he had almost lost his life at the hands of a fanatic. Viscount Aoki and others who followed in the Foreign Office continued negotiations, but demanded terms of equality. The foreign powers found themselves in the position of Tarquin when he was offered the Sibylline Books for a certain price and finally had to pay as much for the one last volume as was asked for the whole set! The concessions offered by Japan grew beautifully less on each occasion and finally were withdrawn entirely; so that the new treaties, when negotiated, left no vestige of extra-territoriality. But that is anticipating the course of events in the next period.

In national political affairs the promise to establish prefectural assemblies was fulfilled in 1880, and these became preparatory schools in political science; and the following year another promise, that of a constitution, was made. The prefectural assemblies do not possess absolute control of the affairs of the prefectures, because they are not entirely independent of the central government. In all cases the final ratification rests with the Governor (who is an appointee of the central government) or with the Department of Home Affairs. The latter also has the power in its own hands of suspending an

---

[1] Providing for only four foreign judges for a few years.

assembly at its discretion. It would seem, then, that theoretically a prefectural assembly in Japan has very little real power of its own. The central government holds the authority to control these assemblies, if it should be necessary; but it also respects local public opinion as far as possible.

In 1889 the right of local self-government was extended to cities, towns, and villages, upon a somewhat similarly centralized system. In cities the Mayor is appointed by the Emperor; and he manages municipal affairs through both a "city council" and a "city assembly," of which the latter is a popular representative body, and the former is elected by the latter. Towns and villages have elective assemblies by which the Mayor and other officials are chosen.

This was a period prolific in the organization of political parties. The honor of establishing the first so-called political party in Japan belongs to Itagaki. He hailed from Tosa, from which it had been prophesied that liberty would come; and he was "the most passionate advocate of the natural rights of man." As early as 1874 Itagaki had organized a political association for the purpose of education in political science. This could scarcely be described, even loosely, as a party, except in embryo.

Another organization of the same kind was called Aikokusha, or "Patriotic Association."

In 1880 an attempt was made to organize a political party "with definite principles"; but it was opposed on the ground that it was premature. However, the Jiyutō, or "Liberal Party," was then organized by Itagaki; and, in 1881, after the Emperor had issued his promise to establish a national assembly, it was reorganized. In 1882 Ōkuma organized the Kaishintō, or "Reform Party," afterward called Shimpotō, or "Progressive Party." In the same year the government supporters organized the Teiseitō, or "Imperialist Party," which was practically the conservative party of that day. In 1886 Gotō tried to organize the various local political bands into a great league, called Daidō Danketsu, the motto of which, expressed in its name, was "similarity in great things, difference in small things"; but his influence and his party were short-lived. These parties were almost all organized around men more than measures, persons rather than principles.[1]

In this way were political parties organized in Japan. But, as the law regulating public meetings was drastic and the police supervision was strict, it was found necessary for them to dissolve in the course of a year or two. However, they were again organized in the next period.

The Liberals, who were Radicals, became dissatisfied with the slowness of political progress, and made such an agitation that, in 1887, many were expelled from Tōkyō by the so-called "Peace Preservation Act," and those who refused to obey were imprisoned. But finally, in 1889, as the climax of the internal development and political preparations, came the extension of local self-government and the promulgation of a constitution, which ushered in the next period.

---

[1] See the author's paper in the July, 1912, issue of the *Political Science Quarterly*.

CHAPTER XIV. THE MEIJI ERA, III

3. *Constitutionalism* (1889-1899). – This period opened, strange to say, with the "anti-foreign reaction" at its height. This reaction was the natural result of the rapid Occidentalization that had been going on, and was strengthened by the refusal of Western nations to revise the treaties which kept Japan in thraldom.

The year 1889 was a red-letter year in the calendar of Japan's political progress. On February 11 was promulgated that famous document[1] which took Japan forever out of the ranks of Oriental despotisms and placed her among constitutional monarchies; and on April 1 the law of local self-government for city, town, and village went into effect.

The Japanese constitution has very appropriately been called "the Magna Charta of Japanese liberty." It was not, however, like the famous English document, extorted by force from an unwilling monarch and a cruel tyrant, but was voluntarily granted by a kind and loved ruler at the expense of his inherited and long-established rights. The late Emperor, in the language of the constitution itself, "in consideration of the progressive tendency of the course of human affairs and in conformity with the advance of civilization," admitted his people to a share in the administration of public affairs.

That important document, at the outset, however, seems far from generous. The Emperor, "sacred and inviolate," is "the head of the Empire," combining in himself the rights of sovereignty; but he "exercises them according to the provisions of the constitution." It is only "in consequence of an urgent necessity to maintain public safety or to avert public calamities,"

---

[1] Drawn up by Count (the late Prince) Itō, Messrs. Kaneko and Suyematsu (now Viscounts), and others.

that the Emperor, "when the Imperial Diet is not sitting," may issue "Imperial Ordinances in place of law." But these ordinances must be approved by the Imperial Diet at its next session, or become "invalid for the future." To the Emperor is reserved the function of issuing ordinances necessary for carrying out the laws passed by the Diet or for the maintenance of public peace and order; but "no ordinance shall in any way alter any of the existing laws." The Emperor also determines the organization of the various branches of the government, appoints and dismisses all officials, and fixes their salaries. Moreover, he has "the supreme command of the army and navy," whose organization and peace standing he determines; "declares war, makes peace, and concludes treaties"; "confers titles of nobility, rank, orders, and other marks of honor"; and "orders amnesty, pardon, commutation of punishments, and rehabilitation." Thus it is evident that the government of Japan is imperialistic, but it is a constitutional imperialism.

The Imperial Diet of Japan consists of two Houses, the House of Peers and the House of Commons. The membership of the former comprises three classes – hereditary, elective, and appointive.[1] The members of the imperial family and of the orders of Princes and Marquises possess the hereditary tenure. From among those persons who have the titles of Count, Baron, and Viscount a certain number are chosen by election, for a term of seven years. The Emperor has the power of appointing for life membership a limited number of persons who deserve recognition on account of meritorious services to the state or on account of erudition. Finally, in each prefecture one member is elected from among the highest taxpayers and appointed by the Emperor for a term of seven years.

The members of the House of Commons are always elected

---

[1] The number is variable – about 375.

by ballot in accordance with the Election Law, by which they now number 381. Their term of office is four years, unless they lose their seats by dissolution of the Diet, as has often happened. "Male Japanese subjects of not less than full thirty years of age" are eligible; but certain officials, as well as military and naval officers, are ineligible. A candidate need not be a resident of the district.

A voter must be full twenty-five years of age; must have actually resided in that prefecture for one year; and must have been paying direct national taxes of not less than 10 yen annually. The present number of eligible voters is over one million and a half (1915).

Some notice must be taken of the rights and duties of subjects under the Japanese constitution. All such persons are eligible to civil and military offices; amenable to service in the army and the navy, and to the duty of paying taxes, according to law; have the liberty of abode, inviolable right of property, right of trial by law, and freedom of speech, writing, publication, public meeting, association, and religious belief, "within the limits of law"; cannot be arrested, detained, tried, or punished, "unless according to law," and can claim inviolable secrecy of correspondence. Moreover, "the house of no Japanese subject shall be entered or searched without his consent," except by due process of law. All subjects may also present petitions, "by observing the proper forms of respect." The freedom of religious belief is granted "within limits not prejudicial to peace and order, and not antagonistic to their duties as subjects."

The constitution recognizes another body, the Privy Council, appointed by the Emperor and consulted by him upon certain matters of state. It consists of about 25 members; and is composed of "personages who have rendered signal service to the state and who are distinguished for their experience," such as ex-Ministers of State and others, whose "valuable advice on matters of state" would naturally be sought. The matters coming within the cognizance of the Privy Council are specified as follows: Matters which come under its jurisdiction by the law of the Houses (of the Diet); drafts and doubtful points relating to articles of the constitution, and to laws and ordinances dependent to the constitution; proclamation of the law of siege and certain imperial ordinances; international treaties; and matters specially called for. The Ministers of State are, ex officio, members of the Privy Council; but although it is "the Emperor's highest resort of counsel, it shall not interfere with the executive."

Naturally, the first decade of constitutionalism was chiefly occupied with the experimental stage, when the relations between the two Houses of the Imperial Diet, between the Diet and the Cabinet, between the Cabinet and political parties, were being more or less defined.[1]

This was also the period during which new civil, commercial, and criminal codes were put into operation; the gold standard was adopted; the restrictions on the freedom of the press and of public meeting were almost entirely removed; and the tariff was revised in the interests of Japan.

In 1889 Prince Haru (the present Emperor) was proclaimed Crown Prince; and in 1891 occurred the attack on the Russian Crown Prince, the present Czar, then visiting Japan.

The most important event of this period, from one point of view, was the war with China in 1894 and 1895. The bone of contention was the mutual relation of the two countries in Korea – the frequent *casus belli* in the Far East. The war began in July, 1894, although the formal proclamation by Japan was not issued until August 1. Party differences, which had become acute, were buried; and the necessary funds for the prosecution of the war

---

[1] See Uyehara, *Political Development of Japan* (1867- 1909).

were voted unanimously.

It is scarcely necessary to go much into the details of the conflict. Unexpectedly to most persons, Japan pursued a practically uninterrupted course of victory, both by land and by sea. After Seoul had been occupied without resistance, one Japanese army defeated a Chinese force at Pingyang in northern Korea, and the Japanese fleet defeated the Chinese fleet off the coast of Korea. The Japanese then crossed the Yalu River into Manchuria, and, winning several victories, advanced even beyond Newchwang and threatened Peking. Meanwhile, another Japanese army, under Ōyama, had landed near Port Arthur, and, defeating every force that tried to make a stand against it, had captured that fortress. Ōmaya then transferred the principal division of his army to the Shantung Peninsula and invested Weihaiwei. When that fortress surrendered, the Japanese land and naval forces combined in an attack upon the Chinese fleet. This resulted in the surrender of Admiral Ting, who then committed suicide. Thus China was compelled to seek peace from Japan. The negotiations for peace were carried on at Shimonoseki between the famous Li Hung Chang and his son on one side and the Premier Itō and the Foreign Minister Mutsu on the other side. The negotiations were temporarily interrupted by an attempt, fortunately unsuccessful, on the part of a Japanese ruffian, to assassinate Li Hung Chang. Peace was finally concluded on April 19, 1895, on the following terms:

> *1. China recognizes the independence and autonomy of Korea.*
>
> *2. China cedes to Japan the Liaotung Peninsula, the island of Formosa, and the Pescadores group of islands.*
>
> *3. China agrees to pay to Japan an indemnity of 200,000,000 taels.*
>
> *4. China agrees to open for Japanese trade certain new cities, towns, and ports and to extend the right of steam navigation for Japanese vessels on the Upper Yangtze River and the Woosung River and Canal.*

But the prophecy of the leading Japanese diviner that "three uninvited guests would come" to the Peace Conference, while not literally, was practically, fulfilled. Russia, France, and Germany interfered, and, declaring "that any holding of Manchuria territory by Japan would constitute a menace to the peace of Asia," kindly (?) *advised* Japan to withdraw her claim to the Liaotung Peninsula. The only two powers that might have assisted Japan against this combination were neither sufficiently interested nor far-sighted enough to interfere; and they (Great Britain and the United States) kept silent. Japan had nothing to do, therefore, but to submit and accept a monetary consideration of an additional 30,000,000 taels for giving up her claim to the Liaotung Peninsula. But therein lay "the germ of the Russo-Japanese War."

The material benefit which Japan received from this war included the acquisition of Formosa and the Pescadores and the receipt of an indemnity which enabled her to prepare for the next conflict, which she knew was inevitable. It needed no special prophetic inspiration to foresee Russia's purpose when she succeeded, with the aid of France and Germany, in robbing Japan of part of the fruit of victory. But the greatest benefit of the war lay in the fact that, while Japan's progress in the arts of peace had not been sufficient to bring acknowledgment of her worthiness to enter the comity of nations, her overwhelming defeat of China at least expedited that recognition. And the result was that in 1894 Great Britain, the United States, and the other treaty powers agreed upon a revision of the old treaties which had maintained the thraldom of Japan, and signed new treaties, which formulated the belated recognition, and were to go into effect five years later.

In educational matters, this period was specially marked by the fact that the Emperor, in 1890, issued an imperial rescript, which has since been the basis of ethical instruction in Japanese schools. The following is the latest official translation, issued by the Department of Education: *Know Ye, Our Subjects:*

> *Our Imperial Ancestors have founded Our Empire on a basis broad and everlasting and have deeply and firmly implanted virtue; Our subjects, ever united in loyalty and filial piety, have from generation to generation illustrated the beauty thereof. This is the glory of the fundamental character of Our Empire, and herein also lies the source of Our education. Ye, Our subjects, be filial to your parents, affectionate to your brothers and sisters; as husbands and wives be harmonious, as friends true; bear yourselves in modesty and moderation; extend your benevolence to all, pursue learning and cultivate arts, and thereby develop intellectual faculties and perfect moral powers; furthermore advance public good and promote common interests; always respect the Constitution and observe the laws; should emergency arise, offer yourselves courageously to the State; and thus guard and maintain the prosperity of Our Imperial Throne coeval with heaven and earth. So shall ye not only be Our good and faithful subjects, but render illustrious the best traditions of your forefathers. The Way here set forth is indeed the teaching bequeathed by Our Imperial Ancestors, to be observed alike by Their Descendants and the subjects, infallible for all ages and true in all places. It is Our wish to lay it to heart in all reverence, in common with you, Our subjects, that we may all thus attain to the same virtue. The 30th day of the 10th month of the 23d year of Meiji [October 30, 1890].*

> *(Imperial Sign Manual, Imperial Seal.)*

In the history of Christianity in Japan,[1] this sub-period may well be called the "Period of Reaction," during which apathy prevailed. The attention of the people was largely given over to political and material civilization; and in Christian circles rationalism and liberalism "chilled enthusiasm" and weakened, even deadened, the spiritual life. And yet it is worthy of notice that in this discouraging period we find the beginnings of such important movements as the Young Men's Christian Association, the Young People's Society of Christian Endeavor, and the National Temperance League. In fact, before the close of this sub-period, there were clear signs that the reaction had spent itself. The climax of the reaction in educational circles was reached in 1899, when the Department of Education issued an Instruction which forbade religious instruction, not only in the public schools, as was perfectly proper, but also in officially recognized private institutions. This, of course, militated very seriously against licensed Christian schools; but it has become practically a dead letter.

In 1899 the new treaties, which threw Japan wide open for trade and residence, and admitted her to the comity of nations on terms of equality, went into effect; and thus began the new period of Cosmopolitan Japan.

---

[1] See Clement, *Christianity in Modern Japan*, and Cary, *History of Christianity in Japan*, Vol. II.

CHAPTER XV. THE MEIJI ERA, IV

4. *Cosmopolitanism* (1899-1910). – It was not so many years ago that the ideal of the Japanese was such a narrow theme as "the Japan of the Japanese"; then the vision widened out so as to include "the Japan of Asia"; but now the horizon is unlimited and extends to "the Japan of the World." Indeed, the Japanese have outgrown "Native Japan," and even "Asiatic Japan," into "Cosmopolitan Japan."

The appropriateness of the title for this period became increasingly evident as the years passed on. In 1900, in quelling the "Boxer" disturbances in China, and particularly in raising the siege of Peking, Japan played a most important part in helping the great nations of Christendom to maintain in China the principles of Occidental, or Christian, civilization. The Japanese troops were officially engaged, together with those of Christian nations, in rescuing Christian missionaries and Chinese converts from mobs; and missionaries, driven out of China, were finding refuge in Japan, where their lives and their property were as secure as in their home lands. Two years later (1902) Japan's claim to be a world-power was still further recognized and thus confirmed by the conclusion of the Anglo-Japanese Alliance, which was itself renewed in 1905 for a further term of ten years. This is the very first instance of the alliance of a white nation with a colored nation. The formerly insignificant and "halfcivilized" country of Japan was now "on the same lotus-blossom" with Great Britain. The huge empire on whose possessions the sun never sets took for its ally the small empire of the rising sun. And the fact that, when Great Britain broke her policy of "splendid isolation," it was to enter into alliance with an Oriental power is one of great significance.

In other matters it is possible to trace the reflex influence of the cosmopolitan spirit. In 1899, for instance, official permission was granted to a Baptist "gospel ship," appropriately named "Fukuin Maru,"[1] to cruise freely among the islands of the Inland Sea, with the Stars and Stripes flying from the masthead. The same spirit was manifested in the hearty welcome given to the late President Charles Cuthbert Hall, the late General Booth, Professor Ladd, and others in their visits to Japan. And it was especially evident in the World's Student Christian Federation, which met in Tōkyō in April, 1907, and was the first international association to meet in Japan. It was composed of six hundred and twenty-five delegates from twenty-five nations.

In 1900 a private woman's university was opened in Tōkyō, and it is now in a prosperous condition.

In the same year occurred the marriage of the (then) Crown Prince to the Princess Sada. And legitimate issue of this monogamic union is found in three sons, born in 1901, 1902, and 1905. Their names are Hirohito, Michi-no-Miya; Yasuhito, Atsu-no-Miya; and Nobuhito, Teru-no-Miya.

The National Exhibition at Ōsaka in 1903 also deserves mention because it widely advertised the material progress of the country.

And now we have reached the time of the great Russo-Japanese War of 1904 and 1905, and are again compelled by the limitations of space to give only the briefest mention to an affair, the details of which are fortunately still fresh in our minds. The remarkable evidences of excellent preparation, as well as the almost unbroken series of victories on land and sea, once more evoked the wonder and admiration of the world.

The Japanese had felt that this war was inevitable. They had seen Russia, by lease, appropriate the Liaotung Peninsula, which they themselves had been compelled to relinquish as one of the

---

[1] *Fukuin* means "gospel," and *Maru* is a suffix which means "ship."

spoils of the successful war with China. They had seen Russian power extend through Manchuria and had encountered Russian designs upon Korea. Unless the "advance of Russia" eastward in Asia should be checked, it meant that Russia would become mistress of the Sea of Japan, and Japan "must forever abandon the hope of winning a position of equality among the great powers." It was "life or death" for Japan.[1]

It was not until after six months of fruitless negotiations that Japan finally adopted the "last resort." She severed diplomatic relations with Russia on February 5, 1904, with a statement that the Japanese authorities "reserve to themselves the right to take *such independent action as they may deem best.*" This was tantamount to a declaration of war.

On the following day Admiral Tōgō left Saseho under official instructions, and, about midnight of February 8, struck the first blow of the war, when six of his torpedo boats attacked the Russian squadron in Port Arthur harbor and inflicted serious damage. The next day Admiral Uriu, with a detachment of the fleet, defeated two Russian cruisers in the harbor of Chemulpo, Korea. Thus the Japanese gained control of the sea and landed troops, who entered Seoul.

The formal declaration of war was made by Japan on February 10, for publication in the newspapers of the following day, which was the anniversary of the reputed founding of the Japanese Empire in 660 B.C. and also of the promulgation of the constitution in 1889. On February 23 a treaty of alliance between Japan and Korea was formally signed at Seoul.

The First Army, under Kuroki, gained its first victory at the Yalu River and then fought its way through Maneburia to Liaoyang. The Second Army, under Oku, landed on the Liaotung Peninsula, and, after bloody contests, got possession of Dalny,

---

[1] See Asakawa, *The Russo-Japanese Conflict.*

the Russian "fiat city." A Special Army, under Nodzu, landed at Takushan and soon united with the First Army. When Nogi came out with the Third Army to invest Port Arthur, Oku's army was sent to check the forces dispatched by Kuropatkin for the relief of Port Arthur.

Meanwhile the Japanese navy had not been idle, but had been busy in attempting to blockade Port Arthur, in checking Russian sorties therefrom, and in watching the Vladivostok fleet. In one of the sorties from Port Arthur the Russian flagship "Petropavlovsk," with Admiral Makarov on board, struck a mine and sank immediately. And a little later the Japanese lost the "Yoshino" and the "Hatsuse."

On August 23 began the Battle of Liaoyang, which lasted for over a week. The three armies of Kuroki, Oku, and Nodzu were united under Field Marshal Ōyama and gained a complete victory. And when Kuropatkin advanced with heavy reinforcements to retake Liaoyang, he was again defeated at the Shaho River. After this the armies practically went into winter quarters.

Thus attention was directed to Port Arthur, where the Japanese had been making general assaults with tremendous losses and had finally resorted to the slower but, safer process of mining.[1] In this way they gradually got, possession of the outer forts, including finally the "203- Meter Hill," from which they had command of the inner harbor of Port Arthur and were able to disable the remnants of the Russian fleet. And on January 1, 1905, Stoessel surrendered Port Arthur to Nogi.

In February, 1905, the armies resumed hostilities, and, from February 24 to March 10, fought the great battle of Mukden, which resulted in a victory for the Japanese. And this victory was largely due to the flanking movement of Nogi's army from Port

---

[1] See Sakurai, *Human Bullets.*

Arthur.

Now Russian hopes centered on the Baltic fleet of Rojestvensky. It had been making its way eastward leisurely and had been enjoying the hospitality of neutral waters. The Japanese fleet, under the indomitable Tōgō, was watching and waiting in the waters between Japan and Korea. And, as all things come to those who wait, to the Japanese came finally the Russian fleet, steering boldly through the Tsushima Channel for Vladivostok. May 27 and 28 (the latter the birthday of the then Empress of Japan) are the red-letter dates of the great naval battle, which resulted in the practical annihilation of the Baltic fleet, with only slight damage to the Japanese fleet. The Battle of the Sea of Japan, as it is officially designated, was the decisive conflict of the war; and it deserves also to rank among the decisive battles of the world's history.[1] If Tōgō had been defeated, the communications of the immense Japanese army in Manchuria would have been severed, and Japan itself would have been at the mercy of the depredations of the Russian fleet. Both Japan and Russia now accepted Roosevelt's proposal for a peace conference. Russia appointed Witte and Rosen (ex-Minister to Japan), and Japan appointed Komura, Foreign Minister, and Takahira, Minister to the United States. They met at Portsmouth, New Hampshire, from August 9 to 29, and finally agreed upon terms of peace. The main points were the following:

1. *Russia recognized Japan's preponderating influence in Korea.*

2. *Russia surrendered to Japan all rights under the lease of the Liaotung Peninsula.*

3. *Russia surrendered to Japan all rights in connection with the Manchurian Railway from Dalny and Port Arthur to Changchun,*

---

[1] This is true because one important result of this battle and this war has been the recognition of Japan as a "Great Power." McCormick, *The Tragedy of Russia*, is one of the best books on the war.

where the two sections should be connected.
4. Russia surrendered to Japan the southern half of Sakhalin.

It is, perhaps, not strange that the Japanese nation was, on the whole, disappointed with the terms of the Treaty of Portsmouth. They had borne heavy financial burdens, and had confidently anticipated at least a partial compensation in the shape of an indemnity and the reacquisition of Sakhalin, of which they considered themselves cheated by Russia in 1875. To get only half of Sakhalin was not so much of a loss, because it was the better half, but to get not one *sen* of indemnity was a bitter pill, without even a coating of sugar. Although most of the Japanese people, as is usual, swallowed their disappointment, agitators utilized the opportunity to stir up the rowdy element to break out in riots in Tōkyō early in September. After the destruction of considerable property, the metropolis was placed under martial law until the excitement subsided. But the wisdom of the Japanese envoys in bringing the war to a close, even on unpopular terms, was fully justified when it soon became evident that the northeastern section of the main island was threatened with a famine, due to the partial or entire failure of crops. And, when the famine did come, the energy which had been spent on the prosecution of the war was at once transferred to the task of relieving the suffering.

The twenty-second session of the Imperial Diet (December 28, 1905, to March 27, 1906) is worthy of notice because it passed, with only slight amendments, the government's bill for the nationalization of the railways of the Empire. And, in the same year, the railways in Korea passed under the management of the Japanese government.

Japan, while martially strong, is also desirous of peace. The Japan Peace Society and other similar organizations are growing in power and influence. The peace of the Far East has been strengthened by the Russo-Japanese Convention and the Franco-

Japanese Agreement of 1907, the Americo-Japanese Arbitration Treaty, the Americo-Japanese Entente of 1908, etc. Japan's pacific policy was also made evident by the cordial way in which she met representatives of Canada and the United States and conferred upon delicate questions of immigration.

In the Christian world of Japan two General Conferences (1900 and 1909) gave a tremendous impulse to the desire for greater co-operation and unity. The widespread "revival" of 1901 and 1902, and the *Union Hymnal* (issued in 1903), were object-lessons of the possibilities along this line. The beginning of the Young Women's Christian Association work in 1904 was the introduction of one more interdenominational effort. And the Standing Committee of Co-operating Missions, now known as the Conference of Federated Missions, has proved itself another most efficient unifying force.[1]

Other significant episodes of this period were the visits of American business men to Japan and of Japanese business men to the United States. The former coincided with the visit of an American fleet to Japan. In welcoming the fleet, the *Kokumin Shimbun*, one of the leading journals of Tōkyō, said: "The sixteen battleships, representative of the noble traditions of American justice, come to our shores as heralds of peace." This was in 1908, and in the fall of 1909 a party of Japanese business men started for a trip to the United States, and returned in the spring of 1910. These visits were most beneficial in both cases, because they gave representative men of both nations opportunities to see the real conditions of affairs in the two countries.

One more important event of this period should at least be mentioned – the completion in 1908 of the railway which runs

---

[1] The annual publication known as *The Christian Movement in Japan* is invaluable. The National Sunday-School Association is another application of Christian unity.

the length of the island of Formosa and is facilitating greatly the development of the resources of that "Beautiful Isle."

Inasmuch as the great prosperity which followed the war led to speculation and extravagance, the Emperor issued an edict of warning to the people (1908).

One shocking event of this period was the discovery in 1910 of an anarchist plot against the "sacred" person of the Emperor. Several were arrested as conspirators and tried by secret trial. A few were acquitted, a few were condemned to imprisonment for terms of years, and twelve were condemned to death and executed (in 1911).

During this period national politics became quite interesting. The Katsura ministry, which established a record by holding office for four and one-half years, was held responsible for the unpopular terms of peace and resigned in December, 1905. It was succeeded a month later by a cabinet under Marquis Saionji, without special change of policy. Saionji had succeeded Itō in the leadership of a new political party, which the latter had organized in 1900, chiefly from the old Liberal party. It was known in full as the Rikken Seiyūkai,[1] but is generally called only by the second name. The Saionji ministry, however, resigned in 1908, ostensibly on account of the Premier's illness, and Katsura again formed a cabinet.

One of the most important results of the Russo-Japanese War has been "the passing of Korea." After the war, as political intrigues did not cease, a Japanese protectorate was established, with Itō as Resident-General; and into his hands passed the control of Korea's foreign affairs. In the following year, by a new agreement, the control of the internal administrative affairs in Korea passed into the same hands. The protectorate then established a "clear differentiation" of the executive and the

---

[1] "Constitutional Government Friends Association."

judicial departments and appointed an earnest Japanese Christian, Judge Watanabe, as Chief Justice of the Supreme Court in Korea. Meantime the Emperor, whose corrupt rule had brought his country to its deplorable condition, abdicated, and was succeeded by his son. The new Crown Prince went over to Japan to be educated; and the Crown Prince of Japan made a visit to Korea (the first instance of a Japanese Crown Prince leaving his native land).

In June, 1909, Itō resigned his position as Resident General, and was succeeded by Sone, who had been Vice Resident-General. In October, Itō was assassinated at Harbin by a Korean fanatic; and he was honored, as the greatest statesman of Modern Japan, with a most elaborate state funeral.

Having been compelled, on account of a dangerous illness, to return to Japan, Sone resigned his post.[1] He was succeeded by Terauchi, then Minister of War, who carried through the plan of annexation, which was formally announced on August 29, 1910 – just five years after the Treaty of Portsmouth. Thus Korea became a "territory" of Japan, with the old name of Chōsen, under a "government-general." This made Japan a continental power.

This "passing of Korea" is a truly unfortunate but inevitable occurrence. It was a practical impossibility for Korea, in her peculiar geographical position, to maintain political independence. The "Poland of the Far East" was destined, not to partition like the European Poland, but to absorption by Russia, or China, or Japan; and she has fallen to the lot of the one best able, probably, to improve her condition.

---

[1] He died September 13, 1910.

CHAPTER XVI. THE MEIJI ERA, V

5. *Continentalism* (from 1910). – In 1910 began a new period, the last one, of the Meiji Era. The annexation of Korea had made Japan no longer an insular, but a peninsular, a continental, power. And, in the following year, the position of Japan, not merely in the Far East, but also in the world-wide comity of nations, was still further strengthened by the new Anglo-Japanese alliance and another revision of the treaties with the Powers.

The revised Anglo-Japanese alliance, to run for a term of ten years, contains a significant provision, inserted in view of the probability at that time of an Anglo-American Arbitration Treaty, that nothing should entail upon either "contracting party an obligation to go to war with the power with whom such treaty of arbitration is in force."

It was in July, 1911, that the term of the treaties which had gone into effect in 1899 expired, and entirely new treaties were negotiated with all the Powers. As these treaties included no limitations upon the commercial autonomy of Japan, they marked absolutely "the end of her extra-territorial embarrassments." And in particular, the new treaty with the United States omitted the objectionable provision of the old treaty, in accordance with which it was permissible for the United States to limit the immigration of Japanese. This delicate question was left to a "gentleman's agreement," by which the Japanese government would exercise the utmost care in granting passports to Japanese to go to the United States.

That year was also distinguished by the generous imperial donation of 1,500,000 yen to start a fund for the relief of the sick poor. This contribution was supplemented by gifts from all over the Empire, until the fund finally reached a total of over

25,000,000 yen. To administer this large amount a society called Saiseikai was organized.

The year 1911 was likewise a red-letter year in the political history of Japan, because, when the Katsura Cabinet resigned, the duty of organizing a new ministry was bestowed again upon Saionji, who made up what was practically a party administration.

One of the most significant events of the year 1912 was what is known as the "Tri-Religion Conference" (in March). It was called by Mr. Tokonami, Vice-Minister of Home Affairs, and consisted of about fifty Shintō, Buddhist, and Christian representatives. It was no attempt to amalgamate those faiths; it was merely a means of bringing representatives together for better acquaintance with each other, for more earnest work in behalf of social and moral amelioration, and for greater emphasis upon the spiritual needs of the nation. The most significant point, however, was the fact that the conference was practically an official recognition of Christianity on the same footing with Shintō and Buddhism.

The trial of a large number of Korean Christians on a charge of conspiring to assassinate Governor-General Terauchi was long drawn out, and complicated by serious charges of torture which shocked the civilized world. It finally resulted in the acquittal of ninety-nine and the punishment of six leaders with imprisonment. It may be added that Japanese judicial processes follow European rather than American models, and are not in accord with Anglo-Saxon ideas of justice.

The most prominent events of 1912 were, of course, the death of the Emperor Mutsuhito on July 30, the accession of the Crown Prince Yoshihito, and the close of the marvelous Meiji Era with the beginning of a new era, called Taishō[1] ("Great

---

[1] *Not* Taisei.

Righteousness"). The limits of space forbid more than the mention of the wonderful scenes, especially in front of the palace, when the prayers of all classes of people, of all religious beliefs, and of no religious belief, were mingled together during those anxious July days and nights.

The imperial funeral was a most elaborate affair, an interesting combination of the old and the new, in which the old predominated; for it was really a Shintō ceremony with some modern Occidental attachments. And the tragic suicide of Nogi and his wife at eight o'clock in the evening of September 13, just as the imperial funeral cortōge was leaving the palace, was in accordance with the old idea of loyalty by following one's master in death. And, while such a course is not in accord with Christian ideas of life and duty, in the minds of the Japanese, on the whole, that suicide was not cowardly or immoral, but a loyal and religious act, which has made Nogi and his wife not only heroes but even "gods."

A few words concerning the personal character of the late Emperor are in place. He is mourned most deeply as a monarch who, in the opinion of his subjects, never made a mistake and performed countless beneficent deeds. He always was kind-hearted and never scolded. He was assiduous in the performance of his imperial duties, and never took a pleasure trip except once to Hakone. He had no favorites, was impartial in his treatment of others, and was not carried away by fads. He invested in the stocks of private companies and corporations, not for the sake of pecuniary profit, but merely to promote business enterprises. With regard to a national policy, he was very cautious in making decisions; but he never wavered in a decision once made. A less broad-minded monarch might have checked the progressive movements of his time. He was always favorable to religious liberty.

The editor of the *Kokumin Shimbun*, in a personal interview granted to the author, emphasized the following points: He was a model constitutional monarch; he always trusted his eminent statesmen, and kept them in their proper places, the right man in the right place; he never deserted his ministers; he was always straightforward and open-hearted. He was never an autocrat, but always welcomed suggestions from the elder statesmen and ministers; yet he was master of the situation and never "dropped the reins." He never signed a law or ordinance without ascertaining for himself whether it was desirable. He was a painstaking, studious monarch; he had a powerful memory, so that his mind was a remarkable storehouse of recent Japanese history, in regard to which he was better posted than many officials. He had great literary talent; his poems were straight from the heart and reminded one of the *Meditations* of Marcus Aurelius. He lived a simple life.

Mutsuhito lived his own name, which means "Friendly [and] Benevolent," and he lived the name Meiji, which means "Enlightened Rule." Mutsuhito lived an arduous but simple life in the strenuous Meiji Era. Therefore, it was most eminently fitting that Mutsuhito "the Great" was given the posthumous name, Meiji Tennō.[1]

But we must devote a little space to the consideration of Japanese art and literature in the Meiji Era, or Tōkyō Period. The results of Western influence upon Japanese art have been twofold, according to Hartmann, who points out the following conditions: first, there is "a new school, based entirely on the art of the West"; and secondly, there is another "new school which, while it works in the old lines and with the old materials, admits the virtues of Western ideas, and endeavors to assimilate them so far as it is able." This makes three art schools in all, which he

---

[1] *Tennō* ("Heaven's King") and *Tenshi* ("Heaven's Son") are common terms for Emperor in Japan.

denominates "the Conservatives, the Moderate Conservatives, and the Radicals." And on the middle school he bases "our hopes in a renaissance of Japanese art." But Okakura, himself a connoisseur in art, thinks that the only outcome must be "victory from within, or a mighty death without."

The recent developments of Japanese literature have been along many lines. Translations from Occidental languages, the rise of a newspaper press and of a magazine literature, new styles in fiction (in which Tsubouchi was the principal promoter of realism), new styles in poetry (in which Toyama was the leader of a movement in favor of longer poems), and new styles in prose, especially along the line of combining the written and the spoken languages, should be mentioned. The increasing popularity of English and other foreign languages, and the persistent movement for Romanization, are factors which must be reckoned in the future development of Japan. The Japanese are an omnivorously reading people, and should be supplied with the best literature. They are eclectic in everything; and, being adept in adopting and adapting, they evolve something unique in every line. The progress of the nation during the Meiji Era may be shown more graphically by contrasting the conditions in certain respects in 1868 and in 1912. In 1868 the whole area of Japan was only about 24,000 square *ri* (about 144,000 square miles); in 1912 it was over 43,000 square *ri* (about 258,000 square miles).[1] The population in 1868 can only be roughly estimated at 30,000,000; in 1912 it was over 66,000,000.1 The figures of the revenue of the state in 1868 are not at hand, and they were only 57,700,000 yen in 1872; in 1912 they were almost 569,000,000 yen, exclusive of Formosa and Korea, which added 91,000,000 yen. In 1868 the foreign trade amounted to less than 26,250,000 yen; in 1912 it ran up to over 1,100,000,000 yen,

---

[1] Inclusive of Formosa and Korea.

exclusive of Korea. In 1868 there was not one mile of railway in Japan; in 1912 there were in Japan, Korea, and (South) Manchuria over 6,300 miles of the "iron road." Similar comparisons might be made with reference to the changes in agriculture, mining, forestry, fishing, industries, manufactures, public works, modes of heating and lighting, architecture, diet, costume, customs, education, language, literature, the press, philanthropic institutions, banking, judicial system (codes, courts, police, prisons, etc.), army and navy, postal service (including telegraphs, telephones, and all modern means of communication), arts and crafts, religion, etc. If another Urashima Tarō (the Japanese Rip Van Winkle) had gone to sleep in 1867 and waked up in 1912, he would have been as much bewildered as either his Japanese or American prototype. And as we contemplate the marvelous transformations of the Meiji Era, we can only throw up our hands with Dominie Sampson and exclaim, "*Pro-di-gi-ous!*"

APPENDIX. PHYSIOGRAPHY

Distances were formerly calculated in miles or a similar measure; but now they must be counted in days or hours. Steam and electricity have so conquered space that linear measure has been superseded by diurnal or horary measure. Moreover, whereas we were taught in geography that a river or a lake or an ocean "separates" one country from another, we should also understand that a river or a lake or an ocean may connect two countries, and even lofty mountains may not be insurmountable barriers.

From this point of view Japan is connected with the United States of America by the Pacific Ocean and is only about ten days distant. And, by the Trans-Siberian Railway, it is about two weeks' distance from England. Japan, therefore, is not difficult of access and is more and more inviting to travelers, to whom she is furnishing ever-better accommodations and ever-greater modern conveniences on sea and land. Her beautiful scenery and interesting people are charms which more and more draw visitors.

Japan is reached from America by several routes across the Pacific. There are various lines of steamers running between Japan and Vancouver, Seattle, Tacoma, Portland, San Francisco, and Mexican and South American ports. The quickest time is made by the Canadian Pacific steamers, the fastest of which make the trip in about ten days. They take a northerly course, where the weather is uncertain, although the steamers themselves are very comfortable. The lines from Seattle, Tacoma, and Portland also take the northerly route. The steamers from San Francisco (and South America) run via Honolulu (or Hilo) by a southerly route, which is favored with more sunny weather but takes a few days longer.

Japan, formerly only an insular nation, has, by the annexation of Korea, become a peninsular, a continental, nation. Insular Japan consists of a long, narrow strip of islands (small, middle-sized, and large), lying off the eastern coast of Asia. It stretches from Kamschatka to the Philippines, from 50° 56' N. to 21° 45' N.[1] It is not strange, therefore, that it is impossible to speak of the climate of Japan as one thing: it is several things, it is almost all things; it is plural – climates, weathers – with big differences within only a few miles. Even Japan proper, which includes Yezo, Hondo ("Main Island"), Shikoku, and Kiūshiu, and lies mainly between the same parallels of latitude as the Mississippi Valley states, presents even more various climates than may be found between Minnesota and Louisiana. And when the Kurile Islands in the extreme north and Formosa in the extreme south are included the extremes cannot meet. And Korea, now Chasen, has its own climate, both similar in some points and different in others. The Kurile Islands, of course, are frigid, and have practically no animal or vegetable life of importance (except seals); while the beautiful island of Formosa is half in the tropics, with a corresponding climate, and abounds in valuable products, like camphor, tea, sugar, salt, tobacco, opium.

Not only the extent of Japan from north to south and the wide differences of depression and elevation, but also the monsoons and ocean currents affect the climate. For instance, the eastern coast, along which runs the Kuro Shio ("Black Stream"), with a moderating influence like that of the Gulf Stream, is much warmer than the western coast, which is swept by Siberian breezes and Arctic currents. Almost all parts are subject to sudden changes of weather.

In general, the climate of Japan is fairly salubrious and on the

---

[1] The longitudinal extent is from 156° 32' E. to 119° 18' E.

whole delightful. The extremes of heat and cold are not so great as in Chicago, for instance, but are rendered more intolerable and depressing by the humidity of the atmosphere. It is also said that there is in the air a great lack of ozone (only about one-third as much as in most Western lands); and for this reason Occidentals at least are unable to carry on as vigorous physical and mental labor as in the home lands. The excessive humidity is due to the insular position and heavy rainfall. No month is exempt from rain, which is most plentiful from June on through September; and those two months are the schedule dates for the two "rainy seasons." September is also likely to bring a terrible typhoon. Except in the northern and western, and in the mountainous, districts, snow is infrequent and light, and fogs are rare. The spring is the most trying, and the autumn the most charming, season of the year.

Japan is a mountainous country. A long range of high mountains runs like a backbone through the main island, and very high peaks abound. Formerly Mount Fuji was literally the "peerless one," on account not only of its beauty but also of its height (about 12,365 feet); but since the acquisition of Formosa, Mount Morrison (about 13,000 feet high) competes for first place on that point. But, in popular estimation, Fuji will always be what a pun on its name makes it – "no second" like it.

Japan is also a volcanic country, with plenty of subterranean fires, which pour out smoke, lava, ashes, and stones from volcanoes, and sulphuric and other mineral water from numerous hot springs. And it is one evidence of the universality of the religious or devout spirit that names like "Little Hell" and "Big Hell" are bestowed upon such places. While fortunately volcanic eruptions are comparatively rare, earthquakes are too frequent. Violent shocks, however, do not come often, but are prone to occur suddenly. It is, therefore, not at all strange that the most unique feature of the Imperial University at Tōkyō is its department of seismology with a seismograph.

On account of both the insular situation and the mountainous character of Japan, there is plenty of falling water, which produces waterfalls, rivers (short and swift), lakes, and swamps. Heavy rains, especially if prolonged, are pretty certain to make the rivers swell and rush impetuously over their sandy banks and cause annually a great destruction of property and a loss of human lives. Tidal waves also are not infrequent. Japan, not unlike Holland, has its constant fight with water, both salt and fresh.

The long and irregular coast line of Japan supplies numerous bays and harbors, both natural and made to order, with shelter for shipping of all kinds. The number of "open ports," where suitable conveniences are provided for foreign trade, had risen from only six in the early days of Meiji to thirty-six at the end of Meiji. The original six are Nagasaki, Yokohama, Hakodate, Ōsaka, Kōbe, and Niigata, the last-named not having been of any special importance in foreign commerce. Of the new ports, Muroran and Otaru in the Hokkaidō; Shimizu (near Shizuoka), Tsuruga, Yokkaichi, and Shimonoseki on the main island; Moji in Kiūshiu; Nawa in Riūkiū; and Keelung, Tamsui, Takow, and Anping in Formosa, have come into importance.

It is a matter of course that fishing and marine industries furnish a means of livelihood to millions of people. But it also follows, as a necessary corollary, that the winds and the waves exact a heavy toll in boats, men, and merchandise. The Pacific Ocean is by no means always as quiet as its name would indicate.

The commonest trees are the pine, cedar, maple, oak, lacquer, camphor, camellia, plum, peach, and cherry; but the last three are grown for their flowers rather than for their fruit or wood. The bamboo, which grows abundantly, is one of the most useful plants, and is extensively employed also in ornamentation.

In the fauna of Japan we do not find such great variety. Fish and other marine life are very abundant; freshwater fish are also numerous. Birds are also quite numerous; and some of them, like the so-called "nightingale" *(uguisu),* are sweet singers. The badger, bear, boar, deer, fox, hare, and monkey are found; cats, chickens, dogs, horses, oxen, rats, and weasels are numerous; but sheep and goats are rare. Snakes and lizards are many; but really dangerous animals are comparatively few, except the foxes and badgers, which are said to have the power to bewitch people! The zoülogical pests of Japan are fleas, mosquitoes, and rats, all of which are quite troublesome; but modern methods have minimized the extent of their power.

Japan proper is divided geographically into nine "circuits," called Gokinai, Tōkaidō, Tōsandō, Hokurikudō, Sanindō, Sanyōdō, Nankaidō, Saikaidō, Hokkaidō. The word *dō,* which appears in all the names except the first, means "road" or "highway," Some of these appellations are not much used at present; but others are retained in various connections, especially in the names of railways, banks, companies, or schools. A common official division of the largest island (Hondo) is into Central, Northern, and Western. Japan was also subdivided into 85 *Kuni* ("Province"), the names of which are still retained in general use to some extent. But, for purposes of administration, the empire is divided into 3 *Fu* ("municipality") and 43 *Ken* ("prefecture"), besides Yezo (or Hokkaidō), Formosa, and Korea, each of which is administered as a "territory" or "colony." The distinction between *Fu* and *Ken* is practically one in name only. These large divisions are again divided: the former into *Ku* ("urban district") and *Gun* ("rural district"); and the latter into *Gun.* There are also more than 50 incorporated cities *(Shi)* within the *Fu* and *Ken.* Moreover, the *Gun* is subdivided into *Chō* ("town") and *Son* ("village").

The area of Japan, not including Korea, is about 175,000 square miles, somewhat larger than Iowa, Illinois, and

Wisconsin; while Korea, with about 80,000 square miles, is larger than Nebraska but smaller than Kansas. While the prefix "Great" does not apply to Japan with reference to its extent, it is certainly appropriate to its elements and features. Within the Empire of Japan are great mountains with grand scenery, great and magnificent temples, great cities, and a great many people. Even in the country districts the villages are almost contiguous, so that it is an infrequent experience to ride a mile without seeing a habitation; and in the large cities the people are huddled very closely together. The latest official statistics (those for 1913) gave the population (exclusive of Formosa, Sakhalin, and Korea) as 54,843,083, of whom the males exceeded the females by about 500,000. If the population of Formosa and Sakhalin be added, the total is more than 58,000,000. The population of Korea is about 13,000,000.

PROVINCES BY CIRCUITS

The following list gives in detail the divisions of Japan into provinces *(kuni)*, according to "circuits."

Go-Kinai *(Five Home Provinces). Yamashiro, Yamato, Kawachi, Izumi (or Senshiu), Settsu (or Sesshiu).*
Tōkaidō *(Eastern Sea Road). Iga, Ise, Shima, Owari, Mikawa, Tōtōmi, Suruga, Kai, Izu, Sagami, Musashi, Awa (or Boshiō), Kazusa, shimōsa, Hitachi.*
Tōsandō *(Eastern Mountain Road). Omi, Mino, Hida, Shinano (or Shinshiu), Kōzuke (or Jōshiu), Shimozuke, Iwaki, Iwashiro, Rikuzen, Rikuchū, Mutsu, Uzen, Ugo.*
Hokurikudō *(North Land Road). Wakasa, Echizen, Kaga, Noto, Etchū, Echigo, Sado Island.*
Sanindō *(Mountain Shade Road). Tamba, Tango, Tajima, Inaba, Hōki, Izumo, Iwami, Oki Islands.*
Sanyōdō *(Mountain Sunlight Road). Harima (or Banshiu), Mimasaka, Bizen, Bitchū, Bingo, Aki, Suwō, Nagata (or Chōshiu).*
Nankaidō *(Southern Sea Road). Kii (or Kishiu), Awaji Island, Awa, Sanuki, Iyo, Tosa (or Toshiu), of which the last four are in the island of Shikoku.*
Saikaidō *(Western Sea Road). Chikuzen, Chikugo, Buzen, Bungo, Hizen, Higo, Hyūga, Ōsumi, Satsuma (or Sasshiu), Iki Island, Tsushima Island, of which all except the last two are on the island of Kyūshiu.*
Hokkaidō *(Northern Sea Road). Oshima, Shiribeshi, Iburi, Ishikari, Hitaka, Tokachi, Teshio, Kushiro, Nemuro, Kitami (all on the island of Yezo), and Chishima, or the Kurile Islands.*
Ryūzkyū *(Loo Choo or Lew Chew) Islands.*

PREFECTURES

The following is the list of Japanese prefectures (*Ken* and *Fu*):

The Fu are three in number – the great municipalities of Tōkyō, Kyōto, and Ōsaka.

The Ken are forty-three in number: Kanagawa, Saitama, Chiba, Ibaraki, Tochigi, Gumma, Nagano, Yamanashi, Shizuoka, Aichi, Miye, Gifu, Shiga, Fukui, Ishikawa, Toyama, Niigata, Fukushima, Miyagi, Yamagata, Akita, Iwate, Aomori, Nara, Wakayama, Hyōgo, Okayama, Hiroshima, Yamaguchi, Shimane, Tottori, Tokushima, Kagawa, Ehime, Kōchi, Nagasaki, Saga, Fukuoka, Kumamoto, Ōita, Miyazaki, Kagoshima, and Okinawa (Riūkiū Islands).The island of Yezo (Hokkaidō), Formosa, Chōsen (Korea) are administered as "territories" by the imperial government, although the first mentioned has recently been granted a small measure of local self-government.

LIST OF EMPERORS AND EMPRESSES[1]

1. Jim-mu (660-585 B.C.).

2. Sui-zei (581-549).

3. An-nei (548-511).

4. I-toku (510-477).

5. Kō-shō (475-393).

6. Kō-an (392-291).

7. Kō-rei (290-215).

8. Kō-gen (214-158).

9. Kai-kwa (157-98).

10. Su-jin (97-30).

11. Su-nin (29 B.C.-70 A.D.).

12. Kei-kō (71-130).

13. Sei-mu (131-190).

14. Chū-ai (192-200).

[Jin-gō (201-269)]

15. O-jin (270-310).

16. Nin-toku (313-399).

17. Ri-chū (400-405).

18. Han-shō (406-411).

19. In-gyo (412-453).

20. An-kō (454-456).

21. Yū-ryaku (457-479).

22. Sei-nei (480-484).

23. Ken-sō (485-487).

24. Nin-ken (488-498).

25. Bu-retsu (499-506).

26. Kei-tai (507-531).

27. An-kan (534-535).

28. Sen-kwa (536-539).

29. Kim-mei (540-571).

30. Bi-datsu (572-585).

31. Yō-mei (586-587).

32. Su-shun (588-592).

33. *Sui-ko* (593-628).

34. Jo-mei (629-641).

35. *Kō-gyoku* (642-645).

36. Kō-toku (645-654).

37. *Sai-mei* (655-661).

38. Ten-chi (662-671).

39. Kō-bun (672).

40. Tem-mu (672-686).

41. *Ji-tō* (687-696).

42. Mom-mu (697-707).

43. *Gem-myō* (708-715).

44. *Gen-shō* (715-723).

45. Shō-mu (724-749).

46. *Kō-ken* (749-757).

47. Jun-nin (758-764).

48. *Shō-toku* (765-770).

49. Kō-nin (770-781).

50. Kwam-mu (782-805).

51. Hei-jō (806-809).

---

[1] Empresses in Italics.

52. Sa-ga (809-823).

53. Jun-wa [Jun-na] (823-833).

54. Nim-myō (833-850).

55. Mon-toku (850-858).

56. Sei-wa (858-876).

57. Yō-zei (877-884).

58. Kō-kō (884-887).

59. U-da (888-897).

60. Dai-go (897-930).

61. Su-jaku (931-946).

62. Mura-kami (946-967).

63. Rei-zei (968-969).

64. En-yu (970-984).

65. Kwa-zan (985-986).

66. Ichi-jō (986-1011).

67. San-jō (1011-1016).

68. Go-Ichi-jō 1 (1016-1036).

69. Go-Su-jaku (1036-1045).

70. Go-Rei-zei (1045-1068).

71. Go-San-jō (1068-1072).

72. Shira-kawa (1073-1086).

73. Hori-kawa (1087-1107).

74. To-ba (1108-1123).

75. Su-toku (1123-1141).

76. Kono-(y)e (1142-1155).

77. Go-Shira-kawa (1155-1158).

78. Ni-jō (1159-1165).

79. Roku-jō (1165-1168).

80. Taka-kura (1168-1180).

81. An-toku (1180-1185).

82. Go-To-ba (1183-1198).

83. Tsuchi-mi-kado (1198-1210).

84. Jun-toku (1211-1221).

85. Chū-kyō (1221).

86. Go-Hori-kawa (1221-1232).

87. Shi-jō (1233-1242).

88. Go-Sa-ga (1242-1246).

89. Go-Fuka-kusa (1246-1259).

90. Kame-yama (1260-1274).

91. Go-U-da (1274-1287).

92. Fushi-mi (1288-1298).

93. Go-Fushi-mi (1298-1301).

94. Go-Ni-jō (1301-1308).

95. Hana-zono (1308-1318).

96. Go-Daigo (1318-1339).

97. Go-Mura-kami (1339-1368).

[Chō-kei (1368-1372)].

98. Go-Kame-yama (1373-1392).

Kō-gon (1331-1339).

Kōmyō (1336-1348).

Su-kō (1348-1352).

Go-Kō-gon (1352-1371).

Go-en-Yu (1371-1382).

Go-Ko-matsu (1383-1392).

99. Go-Ko-matsu (1392-1412).

100. Shō-kō (1412-1428).

101. Go-Hana-zono (1428-1464).

102. Go-Tsuchi-mi-kado (1464-1500).

103. Go-Kashiwa-bara (1500-1526).

104. Go-Na-ra (1526-1557).

105. Ō-gi-machi (1557-1586).

106. Go-Yō-zei (1587-1611).

107. Go-Mizu-no-o (1611-1620).

108. *Myō-shō* (1630-1643).

109. Go-Kō-myō (1643-1654).

110. Go-Sai-in (1655-1663).

111. Rei-gen (1663-1687).

112. Higashi-yama (1687-1709).

113. Naka-mi-kado (1709-1735).

114. Sakura-machi (1735-1747).

115. Momo-zono (1747-1762).

116. *Go-Sakura-machi* (1762-1770).

117. Go-Momo-zono (1771-1779).

118. Kō-kaku (1779-1817).

119. Nin-kō (1817-1846).

120. Kō-mei (1846-1867).

121. Mei-ji (1867-1912).

122. Yoshi-hito (1912-1926).

Nos. 35 and 37 were the same empress; likewise Nos. 46 and 48. In all these lists, names are divided into syllables according to the number of Chinese ideographs employed.

LIST OF SHOGUNS

Mina-moto Yori-tomo (1192-1199)

Mina-moto Yori-i(y)e (1199-1203)

Mina-moto Sane-tomo (1203-1219)

Fuji-wara Yori-tsune (1226-1244)

Fuji-wara Yori-tsugu (1244-1252)

Mune-taka (Imperial Prince) (1252-1266)

Kore-yasu (Imperial Prince) (1266-1289)

Hisa-aki(ra) (Imperial Princes) (1289-1308)

Mori-kuni (Imperial Prince) (1308-1333)

Mori-naga (Imperial Prince) (1333-1334)

Nari-yoshi (Imperial Prince) (1334-1336)

Ashi-kaga Taka-uji (1338-1356 ?)

Ashi-kaga Yoshi-aki (1358-1367)

Ashi-kaga Yoshi-mitsu (1368-1394)

Ashi-kaga Yoshi-mochi (1394-1423)

Ashi-kaga Yoshi-kazu (1423-1425)

Ashi-kaga Yoshi-nori (1429-1441)

Ashi-kaga Yoshi-katsu (1442-1443)

Ashi-kaga Yoshi-masa (1443-1474)

Ashi-kaga Yoshi-hisa (1474-1489)

Ashi-kaga Yoshi-tane (1490-1501)

Ashi-kaga Yoshi-zumi (1494-1511)

Ashi-kaga Yoshi-tane (restored) (1508-1522)

Ashi-kaga Yoshi-haru (1522-1546)

Ashi-kaga Yoshi-teru (1546-1565)

Ashi-kaga Yoshi-hide (1568)

Ashi-kaga Yoshi-aki (1568-1573)

Toku-gawa I(y)e-yasu (1603-1605)

Toku-gawa Hide-tada (1605-1623)

Toku-gawa I(y)e-mitsu (1623-1651)

Toku-gawa I(y) e-tsuna (1651-1680)

Toku-gawa Tsuna-yoshi (1680-1709)

Toku-gawa I(e)-nobu (1709-1712)

Toku-gawa I(y)e-tsugu (1713-1716)

Toku-gawa Yoshi-mune (1716-1745)

Toku-gawa I(y)e-shige (1745-1760)

Toku-gawa I(y)e-haru (1760-1786)

Toku-gawa I(y)e-nari (1787-1837)

Toku-gawa I(y)e-yoshi (1837-1853)

Toku-gawa I(y)e-sada (1853-1858)

Toku-gawa I(y)e-mochi (1858-1866)

Toku-gawa Yoshi-nobu (1866-1867)

LIST OF REGENTS

Hō-jō Toki-masa (1203-1205)

Hō-jō Yoshi-toki (1205-1216)

[Ō-(y)e Hiro-moto (1216-1219)]

Hō-jō Yoshi-toki (restored) (1219-1224)

Hō-jō Yoshi-toki (1224-1242)

Hō-jō Tsune-toki (1242-1246)

Hō-jō Toki-yori (1246-1256)

Hō-jō toki-mune (1268-1281)

Hō-jō Sada-toki (1284-1301)

[Hō-jō Moro-toki (1301-1311)]

Hō-jō Taka-toki (1316-1326)